Jerry Koonce –

Hope through this book
will help you seek God's
will in your life,
　　Thank you for a so
wonderful summer.

The Will of God

Without you, my survival
in Memphis would not
be so fun. Ha! Thank
you. God Bless you
always.

　　　　Your friend
　　　　always,

　　　　David Fain
　　　　July 7, 1984

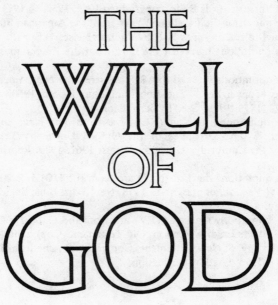

# THE WILL OF GOD

**Morris Ashcraft**

**BROADMAN PRESS**
Nashville, Tennessee

© Copyright 1980 • Broadman Press
All rights reserved.

4216-20
ISBN: 0-8054-1620-X

Dewey Decimal Classification: 231.5
Subject heading: GOD — WILL

Library of Congress Catalog Card Number: 80-65714
Printed in the United States of America

To my wife
Anna Bernice Haley Ashcraft

# Contents

# Foreword

Many people have spoken to me over the years about "the will of God," convincing me of the need for a book on the subject. The handbooks on the subject which I know are practical and helpful but do not deal adequately with the biblical and theological materials. For that reason, I set out to write this volume.

The book is intended for readers who may not have done professional study in biblical and theological subjects. My point has been to translate technical study into the language of the lay reader. I hope the persons who have done formal theological study will not be too disappointed.

I have kept footnotes to a minimum. The bibliography is more detailed and is especially directed toward the larger subject, "the providence of God." The reasons for this will be obvious.

I wish to express gratitude to a number of institutions and persons who have been of help to me in this effort. The Golden Gate Baptist Theological Seminary of Mill Valley, California invited me to give the annual "Derward W. Deere Lectureship in Biblical Studies" in October 1978. I chose the theme "The Providence of God" to give me an opportunity to do more detailed preparation for this study. Those lectures have not been published, but ideas from them appear in these chapters in a different form. The Southern Baptist Theological Seminary of Louisville, Kentucky, invited me to be visiting professor during their Jterm in January 1979, to teach an elective in the field of theology. I taught a course on "The Providence of God" to a class of fifty-five advanced students. This gave me the opportunity of completing the more detailed study and for discussing these ideas with the students. My own seminary,

Midwestern Baptist Theological Seminary at Kansas City, Missouri, has provided me resources and a secretary. Dean Howell and President Ferguson have graciously permitted me to neglect some other duties during the last few weeks while preparing this manuscript.

During the final weeks of revising the manuscript, the Broadway Baptist Church of Kansas City invited me to lead a class in a study on "The Will of God," and members responded to the ideas of these chapters. I am especially indebted to them for this opportunity and to their ministers, Paul Smith, Randy Horn, and Walter Guth for reading the manuscript and offering suggestions.

I express appreciation to my son, Mark Ashcraft, and daughter, Anna Belle Ashcraft, for reading these chapters and offering helpful criticisms. My secretary at the seminary, Elaine Goode, worked overtime several days to type the final draft. Another secretary at the seminary, Debbie Lipscomb, assisted Ms. Goode during rush periods. I acknowledge their help with gratitude.

# 1
# A Conversation—
# Pilgrims Looking for the Way

When you picked up this book, if only to browse, you indicated an interest in this subject. Either you are already a committed Christian or you are thinking about becoming one. Should you decide to read this book, you will be joining me for a while on a journey. As we walk along together, we shall be talking about the will of God. This particular subject may transform our journey into a pilgrimage—travel toward a destination on the basis of religious conviction, faith, and hope. And, we would be pilgrims—not merely tourists.

Yes, you have a right to ask me some questions first. Two of your questions I must try to answer: "Why did you write this book?" and "What does the will of God mean to you personally?" Your third question is such that I think it better if I do not deal with it. You decide that after you have read the book. I must answer your first two questions before you can decide whether or not you are willing to invest the time and effort to read the book.

## Why Did I Write This Book?

More people have asked me more questions about knowing the will of God than about any other subject. In addition to my theology classes in the seminary, I teach in churches, chapels, assemblies, student conferences, and the like. Regardless of the specific subject under discussion, people usually find a way to ask about the will of God. I started teaching at The Southern Baptist Theological Seminary in Louisville, Kentucky, in the fall of 1950. Before that, I was a minister in a church. So, for nearly four decades, this subject has come up frequently. The interest of so many people is my first reason for writing on this subject.

A few of these persons may have been merely curious, but many of them appeared to be really interested. And, to make it challenging, some of them were genuinely concerned. Their own lives were involved. So I have written these chapters for those who are interested and concerned. I hope the curious will read these pages and gain enough interest to become concerned. The will of God is a subject for persons who have a serious and involved attitude toward life. The reader brings his own experiences and beliefs and adds something to what I have recorded.

My second reason for writing is really the answer to your second question, "What does the will of God mean to you personally?" I must give this question more attention in just a moment. But, let me say that the answer to this question comes close to the whole meaning of life as I understand it. To know and do the will of God is human existence at its highest level. Not to know it, or to know it and not do it, seems to me to be a tragic loss.

There is a third reason. The question poses an intellectual challenge. The term is used often in the Bible. Religious people, non-Christian as well as Christian, speak often of the will of God. You and I should be gratified if we can clarify some misunderstanding of the phrase or achieve some additional insight into the will of God.

I suppose I have three reasons for writing: (1) many persons are interested enough to ask about the will of God; (2) knowing and doing the will of God seems to summarize the true meaning of life for me; and, (3) it is an interesting and challenging subject for the student of the Bible and religion.

But, I warn you! Continuing with this conversation may lead you into a deeper commitment of your life than you have heretofore contemplated. You may go too far to back out. The intellectual exercise may bring a small reward of its own, but this is not the kind of information one can learn about and be done with.

I hope you will go with me since I cannot know or do the will of God by myself. In one way, it is the will of God for me individually. But, I cannot know it or do it except in company with other persons. God's will is such that it brings us not only to him but also into closer relationship with one another. We understand his will and do it only in community.

## What Does the Will of God Mean to Me?

Most persons who ask about the will of God are concerned primarily at three points: (1) the will of God as it relates to their individual salvation; (2) the will of God as it relates to purpose, often vocation, in life; and (3) the question about the will of God in times of adversity. These same questions had concerned me since I was a youth, but I have since learned that the will of God involves much more. What I have to say on the subject does relate to research in the biblical and theological areas. However, it also grows out of life experiences. I am not sure but that those life experiences may have shaped my thought as much as the study. Therefore, I owe you a brief statement of that experience. I am reluctant to speak so personally about the will of God for my life. But, since my discussion of the will of God is no doubt colored by my own experience, it seems wise to speak of it.

My parents often spoke about the will of God when they instructed us when we were children. As the fifth of eight children in a Christian family living in rural Arkansas, I heard about the will of God both at home and at church. Mother and Father were not overly religious, but they took their faith seriously. Mother spent her whole life for her family and church. Father was an honest, hardworking carpenter and a deacon in his church. I don't think they were aware of the theological factors involved, but they taught us that God has a purpose for each life and that doing the will of God amounts to doing right. So, prior to my own personal commitment to Christ, I had learned that the will of God gives purpose in life and a basis for ethical living.

An older brother, Charles, had a very wholesome religious experience during his high school years. We understood it as conversion. Later, after some struggle, he announced his decision to become a minister in the church. We spoke of that as a "call" to the ministry. In our region, it was customary to say about such young persons, "he found God's will for his life." His enthusiastic commitment and youthful involvement in the ministry changed our whole family. Our parents and older brother and sisters deepened their commitment; we younger children were moved toward personal decisions of commitment.

Our homelife was happy, despite the hardships of the depression years. We all had good health except my mother who had a heart ailment, the seriousness of which was kept from us when we were young. The four grandparents lived into their mid-seventies and eighties and died at home after very short illnesses. Apart from minor accidents and childhood diseases, there was very little grief in our family during my growing up.

My oldest brother, Quintin, was killed in an automobile accident in July of 1940. His wife survived the accident; their infant son was at home with his grandmother. Of course, we knew that sorrow eventually comes to every home, but we were not prepared when it came to ours. We were all deeply grieved; our family was very close. My mother was crushed most of all. I recall how tenderly my father cared for her during those months. Without any formal education in the area of handling grief, he displayed a remarkable gift born of love. He loved her through it and probably was healed himself in the process.

A family of ten has a host of friends. They were very sympathetic and helpful. They tried to comfort us and it helped. During those days and nights I do recall several of them saying such statements as, "It was God's will"; "God knows best"; "All things work together for good." Some of them phrased questions about the will of God. I did not consider myself a Christian at the time, but I was perplexed by the notion that God had had a hand in Quintin's death.

As the oldest son still living at home, since my father was working away from home at the time, I had to go to the scene of the accident, make the identification, and represent the family until my father returned the next morning. Helen, my brother's widow, kept saying to me that Quintin's last words that night were, "He won't dim his lights." The night was rainy; the highway was wet; the lights were blinding. The other vehicle was a truck with a freight bed extending out beyond the cab. The truck was showing no clearance lights on the bed as was required by law. Apparently, Quintin assumed that the vehicle was a passenger car and moved over to the right enough to avoid it. The truck bed struck his car head-on on the driver's side.

The police at the scene, and the insurance representatives later, explained the accident in terms of driver's error and/or mechanical failure of the lights. So, I knew of these causal or contributing factors. The questions and assurances about the will of God in this situation of grief sounded not only empty to me but also quite unfair to God. I would be very displeased if someone attributed to me a part in a fatal accident unless it was established on the basis of hard evidence that I was, indeed, responsible for it. I was at the age when a boy thinks that men don't cry. So, I didn't. The grief was very deep. It hurt. I did not think it was anger at the time. I know there was a mixture of emotions. For the first time in my life, I felt totally helpless. I don't think I was angry with God. But, I probably was angry with the easy interpretations that blamed God. And, in my dreams, I refused to accept the death as final; Quintin occasionally visited me in dreams, and I kept the secret. And, in my mind, I thought that God was unintentionally blamed for a tragedy he didn't cause by unthinking people who, in their way, were devoted to him.

I became a Christian that same year at age seventeen. I had joined the church at an earlier age but had not known the personal experience of faith we called "new birth." There were many factors involved in this experience. I had heard the gospel all of my life from reliable Christian witnesses and believed that it was true. There were some outstanding Christians in my church and home. They made Christian faith credible. Even before this experience, however, I had come to believe that God had a claim on my life. I had accepted as true what I had been taught: I could not know the real purpose in life until I accepted God's will personally. When I made this commitment, I recall a joyful, calm, and peaceful awareness of reconciliation with God from whom I had felt a distinct estrangement. To me, at that time, this was the first genuine knowledge "of" the will of God; my previous instruction had been "about" God's will.

My call into the ministry came soon afterward. I had planned to go to the University of Arkansas to study law. But, sensing what I thought was a call of God, I went to Ouachita Baptist College instead. I am sure that my decision was influenced by the helpful examples of faculty members and fellow students who appeared to have a high degree of commitment. One of my reasons for going to Ouachita was precisely to have their examples and counsel.

Many would regard my struggle as merely the choice of a life's vocation, but I thought it was the call of God. In the process, I talked with others, questioned, prayed, and reflected. When I decided, I told my pastor, "I think God has called me into the ministry. I think this is the will of God for my life." Many persons will think this impudent, if not preposterous, for a young man of eighteen to think that the God of the whole universe has called him into the ministry. I did not think so because I thought God had initiated it. My pastor did not think me impudent. That experience left me with an urgent sense of purpose in life which has not diminished but has rather increased, despite the customary periods of doubt and discouragement.

Ordination to the ministry was a sacred and memorable occasion for me. The First Baptist Church of Malvern, Arkansas, ordained me later that year. Of course, I was too young, knew too little, had so little experience, but we did it that way in my area. The church trusted me and approved me. Their trust added something to me. I would have been much poorer without that trust which they deposited to my account. I have drawn on those dividends over the years; the principal remains. And, they probably do not realize how much they contributed to my life when they trusted me. Perhaps this is one way God works to achieve his will in our lives. My ordination was not as dramatic as the burning bush experience to Moses or the Temple vision to Isaiah. But, it has been as important to me.

While still a college freshman, I was invited to spend the weekends and summers in a village church as a student-pastor. As I look back upon it, and knowing my inadequacy, I wonder how they endured it. But God entrusted me to the Coy Baptist Church of Coy, Arkansas, just as he had entrusted them to me. They taught me more than I already knew about God and his will. Perhaps churches must on occasions assume the responsibility of raising up a minister. I shall always consider it the providence of God that I was privileged to grow in the fellowship of those small churches in which I served during my college and seminary days. I thought it was God's will.

The United States entered World War II while I was still serving that small congregation. The times were out of joint. Chaos engulfed the nations of the world. Personal lives were fractured. As a minister, I was exempt from military service. But, I could not live with the exemption. I appreciated this arrangement by a friendly government for the churches and their ministers and did not suggest that my colleagues in the ministry do as I did; but in the prevailing circumstances, and as a young man the right age, I thought I should enlist.

Several of my friends criticized me for "turning my back on the call of God." Some of them asked me to justify my action in terms of God's will. My major professor and faculty advisor strongly disapproved. My own personal dilemma at the time has never been completely resolved. The dilemma was that I had a very uneasy conscience about war but was not a pacifist. I certainly did not think the war was God's will. I thought it happened because people would not do God's will. I suppose at the time I was of the opinion that it was the lesser of the evils which confronted us.

My dilemma was intensified by the disapproval of my seniors and peers. A Christian lives in a community and makes decisions in the light of consultation and conversation; one has misgivings when going against consensus. But, in my situation, I thought my decision was right for me. I had difficulty explaining it to others and soon gave up trying. But, though I was reluctant to speak of my decision as the will of God for me, I thought about it a lot. My call to active duty was more sudden than I had been led to expect, and I was denied the opportunity of a face-to-face good-bye to my congregation.

Military service was a strange experience for a young man who had already served as pastor of a church. Many of the young men and women actually enjoyed life severed from the restraints and motivations of home and the civilian community. In spite of the grim purpose for which we were enlisted, I met some other young persons who also knew about the will of God and wanted to do it even in that harsh setting. Of course, I cannot conceive of Jesus flying a military aircraft or otherwise engaged in military missions. Many of us, however, believe that God maintained diplomatic relations with some of us who did. We all know that God does not approve prison camps, concentration camps, and the like; but he seems to have been on rather intimate terms with some of the saints temporarily quartered in them.

There was a kind of ministry even in my new setting. The other men soon learned of my background in the ministry. They gave me numerous opportunities to be their unofficial chaplain-in-residence. I cannot give my statistical summaries, but I did have a feeling that on numerous occasions, in a limited way, I did continue in the ministry.

Several experiences seemed to stress the meaning of the will of God in my life. One happened late in the war. While attempting to land my plane on board the aircraft carrier, I missed the cables and went into the sea. The plane sank in a few seconds; the carrier could not risk stopping for me because of the vulnerability to submarine attack. I had a small rubber inflatable raft and adequate emergency equipment, so the carrier sent a message to a rescue ship and went on. Experiences of this nature were not uncommon; but to the young man waiting in a raft, it was quite significant. As I waited, I reflected. There were no interruptions. My bruises were inconsequential; my reflections were serious, if not critical. It appeared to me that God had been with me. I thought of God's will for my life.

But, my interpretation was an uneasy one.

About three hours earlier another pilot from my group had sunk with his aircraft. We watched helplessly too far away to get to him in time. What about God's will for him? And, then my two high school classmates, Louis Brown and Red Johnson, had perished in similar crashes on the other side of the globe. I knew their mothers; they prayed just as my mother had. So, what about God's will for them? Do you see why we cannot always apply our interpretations about God's will for us to others? We don't know.

When the war was over and I was released from military service, I returned to college and went on to seminary. Seminary days provided a rich period of growth for me. All week long we theological students studied Old Testament, New Testament, church history, theology, ethics, missions, preaching, and so on. Then, on Saturdays we went to our small pastorates to visit, teach, and preach. The combination of a rich, classical, traditional, theological education and practical involvement in ministry is an ideal setting for dealing with the will of God. I cannot express adequately my indebtedness and gratitude to Ouachita Baptist University and The Southern Baptist Theological Seminary for their contributions to my understanding the will of God. All of my teachers were committed Christians—every one of them. The members of the Rocky Ford Baptist Church and Muldraugh Baptist Church of Kentucky contributed greatly to my understanding of the will of God.

I married Anna Bernice Haley of England, shortly before we entered The Southern Baptist Theological Seminary. Our first child, Mark, was born during the early months of my doctoral study. In keeping with the tradition of my family and church, we saw him as a gift from God. We celebrated. When he was twelve weeks old and recovering from minor surgery, he was critically injured in a hospital accident. For several days it seemed that he would not recover at all; then, there was a paralysis on one side of his body. The neurosurgeon feared that the injuries would have permanent effects. Our friends, church members, hospital attendants, and others prayed for him. Finally we were allowed to take him home;

he was still in a cast. We waited. In time, he began to improve daily. Our hope increased. In a few months we were convinced that his recovery was complete. And, it was. To the best of my memory, we were not bitter. We had no ill-will toward the student nurse who had been responsible for the accident. Why should we have? I do not recall any questions about the will of God in this event. I do confess to some resentment toward the hospital officials who seemed to place their legal interests before persons.

Bernice and I sensed the presence of God sustaining us and our son during the experience. We believed that Mark's recovery was related to the prayers offered for him as well as to the care given him by the physicians. We expressed our gratitude. Does it make sense to believe that the will of God was not involved in the accident but was involved in the recovery? Yes, indeed!

Our second son was ill several times during his brief life. The physicians could not diagnose the exact cause of his repeated infections. During his last three-week stay in the hospital, he lapsed into a coma which deepened for eleven days. The kind, Jewish urologist could not tell me directly what was happening that morning. But, he showed me the temperature chart which the nurses had kept during the night. Each hourly notation showed a lower body temperature. He spoke through very visible tears, "I lost three of my own children," and walked out of the room. I phoned Bernice who had gone to our apartment to rest and refresh while I had taken the night watch. She returned to the hospital, and we just sat with our son during those last hours. The same qualified medical specialists had worked over him; the same people had prayed; the same God had listened. We sensed the presence of God as clearly during the loss of Jeorge as we had during the previous recovery of Mark. Mark is now a thirty-year-old associate professor of psychology; Jeorge is like a flower that bloomed in our lives for a short eighteen months over twenty-five years ago.

I ask you to talk with me about the will of God. In that experience, we did not voice the questions, Why did it happen this way? Why did it happen to us? These questions may be inappropriate.

The medical doctors can give you a causal explanation in terms of factors that result in death. But, that is a different kind of question and answer.

Grief is an experience of life. But, that doesn't mean that God sends it. Perhaps it results from many complex factors, many if not all of which are of human making. The question that becomes appropriate is, What should I do in this situation? or What is the will of God for those of us who remain? My wife realized that her other son and daughter Anna Belle, who was born a year later, needed a cheerful home and a happy mother. She dealt with her grief with the resources God had given her and believed the will of God for her was to be the best wife and mother she could be for her family.

During the last months of my graduate study, I served as a temporary instructor in the seminary. I had planned to be a pastor, not a professor. After completing my graduate degree, I was invited to join the faculty of The Southern Baptist Theological Seminary. Again I prayed, reflected, and consulted with persons who knew me well. Slowly, a conviction developed that I should invest my life in the theological classroom. To me, this seemed to be the will of God.

On a cold January day in 1956, I stood in the chapel of the seminary and signed my name to "The Abstract of Principles" in the presence of several hundred witnesses. That document had been written in 1859 by Basil Manly, Jr., one of the founders of the seminary. The public signing of the doctrinal statement formally marks the beginning of the teaching career of a professor on a theological faculty. It is like ordination. In my case it was a deep emotional experience. I thought it was the will of God for my life.

A seminary professor enjoys a great privilege as well as a heavy burden. It is an honor to be entrusted with the education of the ministers and missionaries by the church. But it is a humbling burden for which no one is fully able. The last twenty years have been spent as a professor of theology in Midwestern Baptist Theological Seminary. In addition to the seminary classroom, I have a continuous ministry in the churches. For me, this is living in the will of God. This is my interpretation. Other interpretations are possible. It is just possible that I may be cluttering up the ground, occupying a chair of theology which should be held by a more competent person. I have to reckon with that too.

The meaning of life, as I understand it, is derived from a relationship with God and with those persons with whom we live the Christian life in this pilgrimage. While we cannot know fully what his will for us is at the beginning, we can come to know more about it along the way.

We can talk more meaningfully about the will of God in retrospect. If so, we shall understand the will of God for our lives in direct proportion to our involvement in the pilgrimage. So, we should be on the way.

### Preliminary Definition

Perhaps we need a brief working definition. What does *will* mean? The word *will* is like the word *love*; it is a word with meaning only in a personal context. How can you define *love* except in terms of a lover and a beloved? We understand when we say, "Paul loves Cindy," or "the mother loves her baby," or "God loves me." Then, after defining the transitive verb *love*, we can use the noun *love* with meaning and be understood because we see the relationship between the subject who loves and the subject who is loved.

When we speak of the will of God, let us also remember that the personal God "wills" for personal men, women, and children. Then *will*, as a noun, is the personal intent or purpose which God desires or wishes. It always designates a personal relationship—it is never a legalistic or rigid plan. Many of us miss the meaning of the "will of God" because we depersonalize the phrase and try to use it in an abstract sense.

The persons for whom God has a will also have wills of their own. *Will* is a part of our personhood. God, the Creator, gave us our wills. Although we are capable of turning our wills against God, the Scriptures are clear that God does not coerce or manipulate our wills. He teaches, persuades, and leads us; but he respects the integrity of our wills. He created us this way. Not only does God refuse to coerce or manipulate our wills but he also teaches us not to coerce or manipulate other persons. This leads us to the awareness of the responsibility that attends our wills in their freedom.

We are responsible to God and to others for the wills entrusted to us. We can say no even to God. God does not force our no into a grudging yes. Although God may instruct us, persuade us, and seek to lead us, we can exercise our wills against him. And the consequences can be serious—I think, eternal. We are deceived, or we deceive ourselves, when we deny this responsibility by thinking that ultimately everything works out according to God's will. That view is called *fate*.

Fate is a popular belief in the Islamic religion. It is a foreign word and has no place in Christian usage. A Muslim speaks often about the will of Allah. Believing that all things have been previously determined by Allah, he accepts prosperity or adversity with resignation, "Allah willed it."

In Christian understanding, the will of God is not fate. We do not do the will of God in grudging resignation. God has a glorious purpose for us. This purpose challenges us to our most dedicated commitment; it comes with joy. But some Christians settle for a version of fate.

A certain religious man of long ago, named Akiba,[1] went on a journey carrying a lamp and a cat and leading an ass. When nightfall approached he requested lodging in a village. But, the villagers refused him. So, he said, "Whatever God does, he does for good." Then, being a patient and hardy man, he went into the open desert and camped for the night. But, his trouble had only begun. Adversity followed on the heels of rejection. During the night, a gust of wind blew out his lamp; a desert dog killed his cat; and, a lion ate the ass. But Akiba was a religious man. He said again, "Whatever God does, he does for good." When morning came, Akiba learned that the inhospitable villagers had also had misfortune. A roving band of raiders had attacked the village during the night, killing many and taking the survivors captive. But, Akiba upon learning of their unpleasant experience, commented, "Did I not tell you, God does all that he does for good?" There are some contemporary Christians whose theology sounds a lot like Akiba's.

## The Place to Begin

If Jesus Christ is really the Son of God, as I believe he is, and if the Gospels really tell us about him, as I believe they do, then our first concern should be to learn what Jesus taught about the will of God.

It may seem unnecessary for me to point out the importance of biblical study and Jesus' teaching as the starting point. But, think of how many people discuss the will of God without following this procedure and the confusion that has resulted.

Christian faith is grounded in the event of Jesus Christ. Christians believe "that God was in Christ, reconciling the world unto himself" (2 Cor. 5:19). We believe that he is the fullest revelation of God. In Christ we see what God the Father is like and what we ought to be like. The New Testament is composed of writings which deal explicitly with Jesus Christ and the Christian faith which emerged in response to his life, death, and resurrection. We Christians believe the Old Testament is vitally related to the New Testament and prepared the world for Christ's coming. So, the Bible is always the primary source of information about faith for Christians.

But the Bible is a large book. It is very diverse in its contents—history, poetry, drama, parables, Gospels, apocalypses, and so forth. Is there a unity within the diversity? Christians believe that Jesus Christ, the culmination of God's redemptive work, is the one who gives the Bible unity. So, we see Jesus Christ as the clue toward understanding the teachings of the Bible. We certainly believe Jesus Christ is the clue toward understanding God.

If Jesus Christ is the one who gives meaning and unity to the Bible, does it not follow that we should go to him first in our attempt to learn what the Bible teaches about the will of God? To be sure, there are certain presuppositions involved in this method.

But, unless we know the biblical teachings, we are likely to misread the other signs about the will of God we may encounter along the way.

Our journey is like a migration across the continent or a voyage across the sea. We need one constant, something that does not vary, to guide us. The bedouins who travel the deserts and the sailors who cross the seas have looked up to the stars and constellations. In the northern hemisphere there is one star, Polaris, that remains "fixed" in its place. It is at the end of an infinitely long imaginary line running through the earth from south to north pole. The North Star enjoys one other advantage; the Big Dipper revolves around it and always points toward it. Even a novice can locate it. It is not as bright as Sirius of the constellation Canis Major; Sirius is the brightest star in the heavens. But, Polaris points the way.

For a short journey, one may need only the star, Polaris. But those who cross the deserts and oceans have learned that other stars and constellations are in orbit as clusters with a measurable relationship to Polaris. These others help to check one's position. A celestial navigator can operate from sightings and measurements from two such bodies. But, if one locates three, he can know his position exactly. Then one can navigate with great confidence and accuracy.

Jesus Christ is our North Star. You recall also, that he, too, is surrounded by a number of other stars and constellations, persons and events, which are in orbit in relation to him. He is always the center; they provide additional guidance. The navigator of the ship at sea looks for as many of these guides as he can locate; they confirm or correct his previous calculations. You and I are not going just across the sea, but all the way. Let's do it right!

We will go to Jesus Christ first; then we shall go to Paul and the other biblical authorities who speak on the will of God. If the biblical study seems a bit heavy, think of it as a lesson in navigation that will be essential for the rest of the journey. The goal will more than justify any difficulty we encounter. Let's go!

# 2
# Jesus—
# Our Father . . . Thy Will Be Done

*Our Father who are in heaven, hallowed be thy name. Thy king-
dom come, Thy will be done, On earth as it is in heaven (Matt. 6:9).*

How do you speak about God? When you speak to others about
God, do you feel hesitant or unsure of your language? Perhaps
this reluctance is itself an evidence of your idea of God's holiness.
The ancient Hebrews refrained even from voicing the proper name
of God; they used another word like *Lord*. We should speak of
God with reverence, awe. God is holy. But we must speak of God.
How can we speak of God?

Jesus spoke of him as Father. This is not a peculiarity growing
out of his particular sonship; he taught his disciples to address God
as, "Our Father who art in heaven." When informed Christians
pray to God, they say, "our Father"; when they speak about God,
they say, "God, our Father," or "the God and Father of our Lord
Jesus Christ" (Eph. 1:2-3).

It is important for us to indicate how we speak of God and our
understanding of God in order to be understood when we speak of
the will of God. We are grateful to the philosophers of the ages who
have reasoned about God and have taught about him. We have a
special indebtedness to the inspired witnesses of the Old Testament
without whom much of our New Testament information would not
be clear. But, for Christians, Jesus Christ is the starting point. He is
uniquely Son of God and the fullest historical revelation of God (2
Cor. 5:19; Gal. 4:4-6; Col. 1:15-20; John 1:1-14). If Jesus Christ is
our clearest revelation of God, then we go to him first in our attempt to understand the will of God.

Jesus' life and teachings clarify the will of God at many points. For our discussion, let's look at the following: (1) In prayer, God is "our Father," and the holy Father; (2) the will of God is "thy will"; (3) Jesus knew a struggle between "my will" and "thy will"; (4) Jesus saw his whole purpose in life in terms of the Father's will; (5) he related our salvation to God's will; (6) he spoke clearly of the human response to the will of God in the case of the unwilling; (7) he dealt with questions about the will of God growing out of adversity in life.

### Our Father Who Art in Heaven

Jesus spoke of God as Father. This designation for God had been used a few times in the Old Testament (Isa. 63:16; Ps. 103:13; Deut. 32:6). It had also appeared a few times in Greek literature and in later Judaism. But, Jesus used it in a distinctive way and thereby spoke about our relationship to God. The use of *Father* as a name for God implies a family bond with its closeness and intimacy, but reverence for God is not lost in familiarity.

*The first major clue toward understanding the will of God is Jesus' use of the phrase "our Father."* It reminds us that we stand before God as a family—"our Father"—and not merely as individuals. Our Father is personal and loving; we do not believe in an impersonal divine principle. We speak to God as "thou" and "our Father" and not merely "about" him. This understanding of God holds us in a personal relationship with him. The will of God for us, then, is that personal purpose he wishes for us. It is God's "good pleasure." Through Christ we know that God loves us infinitely more than a parent loves a child and purposes for us, both individually and collectively, what is good.

God's will for us stresses his intent or goal for us. God's purpose in creation is spotlighted in his intent for us whom he created in his image. He gave to us a nature distinct from the other creatures. He intends for us to be creatures who develop the talents with which we are endowed. Our possibilities extend beyond the imagination of most of us; God intended that we dream, hope, plan, work, aspire, and live into the future. He endowed us with a freedom which opens these possibilities. It is his will, his intent, that we not only explore them but also have dominion over them.

It is God's will that we remain in the personal relationship with him and other persons as "I-thou" or even better "we-thou," as expressed in the phrases "our Father." In thinking of the will of God, we are reminded that he is the personal heavenly Father, and we are personal creatures. We should object to every depersonalization, whether of God or of human beings.

The will of God for us may well be in keeping with that which we love most and enjoy most. When my son entered college, he intended to study medicine. He had been encouraged by a high school counselor. At the end of his freshman year, however, he changed his major to psychology. He wrote me to explain why he had done so. He seemed to think that I might have considered his change of vocation a failure. Rather, I was happy that he had recognized on his own the aptitudes and inclinations of his life and had made his decision. I wanted for him a lifework which would bring him joy and a sense of achievement and contribute to the well-being of the human family. My wishes for him included his own free decision— his will. Where did we get the idea that God's will for us is different from our capabilities and talents?

The understanding of God as Father determines for us an understanding of creation. It may be merely "the world" to others; to us, it is our Father's creation. So, we cannot view it as a giant machine operating of itself blindly; we see it as God's creation in which he maintains by his providence a sustaining and guiding role. We do not deny the fact of evil, but we believe in God's continuing presence. Then, if it is God's good creation, we the creatures are not billiard balls on a table moved when struck by a cue stick or another ball bouncing off the cushions; we are persons, created in the image of God with wills of our own. We do not merely react to our environment as if we were animals or chemicals; we respond after we have reflected with our own minds. Evil confronts us not only as a theoretical problem and opponent of our faith in God but also as a practical scourge which threatens to destroy us. But faith in God holds us to him in hope. As creatures with wills of our own, we cannot accept the surrender into being "merely world."

This belief in God as "our Father" precludes the idea of impersonal fate. Fate is an alien word; it suggests a determinism, a fixedness, an ironclad scheme set in concrete, which coerces persons into an inevitable pattern. Such a closed system of reality is appropriate neither for God nor men and women. "Our Father" is the Creator.

### Hallowed Be Thy Name

Even Jesus could not address God without the awareness of God's holiness. God is heavenly Father, but God is holy. In his presence we bow, fall to our knees, or even on our faces. He is God; we are creatures.

Moses stood in the presence of God before the burning bush. The sacred presence transformed that place into "holy ground." Moses removed his sandals in recognition of the holy God in whose presence he stood in wonder (Ex. 3:5).

Isaiah, in the Temple, bowed in reverence and awe when he realized he was in God's holy presence. He sensed his own unworthiness, sinfulness, and creatureliness in the presence of Creator. God is holy! Holy! Holy! Holy!

The word *holy* means other. It designates that quality which only God has. It is his distinctive majestic godliness.

Saul of Tarsus knew about God and about Jesus of Nazareth. On the road to Damascus, however, there was a light and a voice and a vision of the risen Lord. In that holy presence, Saul could only say, "What will you have me do, Lord?" Note "Lord." He engaged in no frivolous discussion about God in the third person! "Lord" is a word of confession and obedience: second person, address, personal address. God is holy! In his presence, we creatures bow.

There are those who approach the study of the will of God as if God were a vocational counselor whose job it is to help us find out what we should do in life, and then, having told us, let us go on our happy, pagan ways. There are others who think that God is our "supplier of needs" who sits at a switchboard in heaven like a dispatcher to hear our requests and answer them. Not long ago, a church person actually said to me something like, "It's God's business to hear our prayers and do something about the world situation."

Those who know God, like Jesus does, address him as Father. Then, they say, "Hallowed be thy name!" for "thou art God, the holy One."

If we talk about the will of God, we must be clear about the "God" whose will we discuss.

## Thy Will Be Done on Earth as It Is in Heaven

Jesus implied in this statement: (1) God does have a purpose for his creatures and creation; (2) his will is being done in heaven (presumably, that is what makes it heaven); (3) his will is not being done on earth as it should be; and, (4) believing in God disposes one to desire that God's will should be done on earth as it is in heaven.

The purpose of God is clarified in the statement, "Thy kingdom come." The kingdom of God, or heaven, is the reign of God acknowledged by his creatures. In a sense, the kingdom is present now; in another sense, it is future. That is why we should pray "Thy kingdom come." We have already come to know him as King; his kingdom is real to us; we accept his reign partially. Now, we pray that it will come more completely in us and in others.

We assume that heaven's standard, God's reign universally accepted with joy, should be earth's standard. This is the same as believing in God. This is the meaning of faith.

Faith is the human response expressed in this prayer, "Thy will be done on earth as it is in heaven." Faith does not mean that we hold a certain opinion about God; it is not even a conclusion about God. Either would reduce God to an object of knowledge. Faith is a personal trust in God on the basis of knowledge. As such, it is a commitment of one's life to God. So, believing in God, we desire that his reign shall be more completely acknowledged on earth as in heaven. Believing in God puts us on his side. Believing in God transforms the world into creation, *God's good creation*. And, this endows it with purpose and meaning. As people who believe in

God, we want his will known and acknowledged on earth. We want all people to know this faith in God.

Of course, the limitation of language requires us to speak of God and of God's will in the third person as I have been doing. But we shall distort it less if we frequently use the wording of the prayer as address in the second person, "Thy will."

This view of the will of God reinstates obedience as a cardinal Christian virtue. Many of us in the modern world have been nourished on "rugged individualism" which often runs close to a lawless outlook in life. We assert a pagan view of human freedom and demand rights which we cannot handle. The word *obedience* sounds weak in this mind-set. But, it is not a weak term in the New Testament. Rudolf Bultmann, a German New Testament scholar and theologian, sees all Christian ethics as a matter of "radical obedience." It is the personal obedience to Jesus Christ and his way of living. Many people think Bultmann is a heretic, and I find his view of the historical nature of the Gospels too radical, but he knows the Christian spirit of obedience.

Obedience is a beautiful word in a Christian setting. It is the deep and joyful attitude of wanting to do God's will and wanting others to do God's will. We obey him because we have come to know him and we believe in him.

Now, we cannot grasp the meaning of the will of God unless we are grasped by the spirit of obedience. Our individualism has led us to neglect our community responsibility, our church relationship, and to disrespect legitimate authority. In our generation, lawlessness is considered a virtue; and criminals are our heroes; many citizens side with the lawbreaker against the police. The clamor for individual rights at the expense of the community is the essence of sin, self-exaltation.

Obedience is the true spirit of the Christian. Obedience is not mere compliance with religious rules. Rather, it is an intelligent acknowledgment and joyful acceptance of God's disclosed will— just because it is right and good. Obedience is neither grudging surrender nor resentful acquiescense. Instead, it is joyful living in accord with the will of God who created the whole universe.

For instance, did you ever hear an astronaut complaining about having to obey the laws of nature? He has spent years studying what others have learned about the physical universe—the so-called "laws of nature." These are not arbitrarily imposed rules for our discomfort or inconvenience. They are the warp and woof of the universe. They not only hold it together; they are the universe. The astronaut knows that he needs a maximum amount of thrust to get free from the gravitational pull of the earth in his thrilling outward journey; but he does not want that law of gravity repealed for him. It may resist his departure, but it is his only hope of return. He does not ignore, violate, defy, or resent it; he obeys it. How childish can we be? Obedience is a mature and disciplined attitude based on knowledge, reflection, appreciation, and action. The Christian joyfully joins Jesus in praying, "Thy will be done!"

In speaking about the will of God, we need to be guided by Jesus' statement in the Lord's Prayer.

## Not My Will—Thy Will Be Done

And going a little farther he fell on his face and prayed, "My Father, if it be possible, let this cup pass from me; nevertheless, not as I will, but as thou wilt" (Matt. 26:39). In the prayer in Gethsemane, Jesus drew attention to a contrast between "my will" and "thy will." This is a crucial distinction both for what it means and what it does not mean.

It does not mean a rejection of his own will, nor a surrender of his will. He was not depreciating his own will. Without "my will" neither Jesus nor anyone else would be a person. One cannot do "God's will" except by a decisive act of a "my will." The understanding of the contrast of "my will" and "God's will" may be next in importance to our understanding of the nature of God.

In Gethsemane, the grim shadow of the cross intensified the darkness of the night until even Jesus temporarily lost sight of the will of the Father, his purpose in life. When we lose sight of God's will, our will comes to the center. And, Jesus knew the symptoms and the dangers.

His prayer in Gethsemane reveals again what he had disclosed in the temptation at the beginning of his ministry: (1) Jesus had and retained his own will, "my will"; (2) he respected the Father's will as the ultimate purpose in life; (3) he had temporarily lost sight of it; (4) evil is real and dangerous and appears in the temptation to do "my will" instead of God's will; (5) victory came when he saw the rightness of God's will and willed to do it; (6) and, other wills were also involved.

The temptation of Jesus poses a number of difficult questions, but several factors are clear. Temptation is not sin; it is an enticement toward it. Jesus' temptations were to achieve God's kingdom in the wrong way. Then it would not have been God's kingdom. The temptation was prolonged and intense (Matt. 4:1-17; Luke 4:1-13). Jesus won a victory over his temptation not by a surrender of his will but by a courageous and intelligent use of it. He chose to go the way of God who created the universe.

Jesus lived and taught out of the conviction that God gave human life its purpose and direction. He said, "For I have come down from heaven, not to do my own will, but the will of him who sent me" (John 6:38). His genuine humanity is obvious in the contrast of "my will" and "God's will." God's will is our ultimate guide; "my will" is my own personal existence.

When Jesus lost sight of the Father's will, his own will came to the center. This happens to us. We were created as creatures to live in community with one another. Knowing and doing God's will holds us to God and keeps us rightly related to one another. When we lose sight of God's will and focus on "my will," we introduce unmanageable conflict within ourselves and within the human community. Neither you nor I, however, surrender "my will" when we join each other in doing the will of God who made us both. We actualize "our wills."

"My will" should not be the center of my life. We are creatures. When Adam and Eve turned away from God's will to do their own—self-exaltation—they turned against the whole creation. Sin may be spoken of as, "we have turned every one to his own way" (Isa. 53:6). To be a Christian, Jesus indicated that one could not have "self" on the throne; God must be the Lord (Matt. 16:24).

Jesus appeared strong, courageous, and distinctively a "self" when he walked out of the wilderness and out of Gethsemane. When he resolved the conflict between his own will and the will of God he lost nothing; he did not surrender; he was victorious. His will did not merge into the Father's will nor was it rejected. It was his will that decided to be faithful to his purpose in life, to do God's will.

Other wills were involved in Jesus' temptations. It was not a drama with two actors—God and Jesus. Neither was it a drama with three actors—God, Jesus, and Satan. It was not a drama at all; it was a real historical situation. In addition to the participants named above, there were many others: the twelve disciples, the priests, the soldiers, the mob, the unborn generations, you and me. It is never merely "my will" or "God's will." All of the other wills are also involved directly or indirectly. When you and I decide, we need to recognize these others who are involved; that is why we want to know God's will. God represents what is good for all of these others.

Choosing God's will over our own wills when there is conflict is not surrender; it is victory. Jesus knew no grudging acquiescence to the Father. His own will accepted as right that which was the Father's will. Musicians in a symphony do not consider it surrender of their will when they follow the conductor; they realize their purpose precisely in their following. Stubborn resistance to God's will is not the expression of genuine human freedom. Rather, it acknowledges servitude to another and alien will.

## The Will of God as the Purpose and Meaning of Life

New Testament scholars often point out that the entire focus of Jesus' life was related to "the will of God." Kümmel believed that the entire proclamation of Jesus was the proclamation "of God's will."[1] Rudolph Bultmann stated that Jesus attempted to correct the legalism of his day by stressing personal obedience to the will of God.[2]

Jesus indicated that doing the will of God was his total purpose in life. It was the source, goal, substance, and meaning of life.

We human beings cannot really live without purpose. The stronger our reason for living, the stronger is the person. Even nonreflective and inarticulate persons give evidence that this is the case with them. For Jesus, this whole purpose had to do with the will of God. God's will was the *whence*, the *whither*, the *what*, the *who*, and the *why* of life. Ask a person these five questions and you will know if he or she has a purpose.

Jesus indicated the will of God as the origin, the *whence* of life. "For I have come down from heaven, not to do my own will, but the will of him who sent me" (John 6:38). The person who has been sent has a mission. When the sender is God, a person has a motivating purpose in life. You and I are here by the will of God. The Christian doctrine of creation, as taught in Scripture and cherished by the church, means that we are here by God's will. We know about biology and inheritance, but we speak of an ultimate origin in God's will.

Meaningful life not only speaks of an origin, a *whence*, but also of a goal, a *whither*. Jesus lived as much out of the power of the future as out of his origin. He said,

And this is the will of him who sent me, that I should lose nothing of all that he has given me, but raise it up at the last day. For this is the will of my Father, that every one who sees the Son and believes in him should have eternal life; and I will raise him at the last day" (John 6:39-40).

Jesus' life was empowered by a conviction that he worked toward a future goal according to God's will.

In evaluating persons for employment or promotions, we look at their "track records," as if they were race horses and not people. We think we can evaluate their future potential and performance in terms of their past achievements. There is, of course, some validity in this principle. But, consider how much more accurate we would be if there was a way to know the person's hopes or goals. We would meet a young man or woman with the question, "Where are you going?" or "What is your goal in life—your whither?" And that would tell us who the person is.

The will of God was the very substance—the *what*—of Jesus' life. It was the substance of his life mission (John 6:38-40). When he was told that his mother and brothers were outside inquiring about him, he responded, "Who are my mother and my brothers?" (Mark 3:33). Then, looking at the crowd, he said, "Here are my mother and brothers! Whoever does the will of God is my brother, and sister, and mother" (vv. 34-35). Jesus was not indifferent toward his family. He loved them. But God's purpose moves even beyond immediate family. We see ourselves most clearly when identified as persons related to others. This tells us who we are.

Jesus indicated that the purpose—the *why*—of his life was related to the will of God. "My food is to do the will of him who sent me, and to accomplish his work" (John 4:34). The harvest was ready; the task was urgent; even physical hunger paled when Jesus thought of the *why* in his life. An unseen and unexplained source of energy sustained him, his purpose.

Viktor Frankl, a Jewish psychiatrist incarcerated in a concentration camp during World War II, learned the power of purpose. He noted that those people who had a strong reason for living could endure more; they lived longer on less. Those with less reason for living gave up more quickly; they died. He survived it all because each morning he looked for something he could do during the day that would help someone else. He found a reason for living. He developed a new method of therapy based on this discovery. He wrote that a person could survive almost any *what* in life if that person had a real *why* for living. For Jesus and those who follow him, the *why* is the will of God. What a motivation for living!

## Our Salvation Is God's Will

You may think that this is so obvious that the mention of it is unnecessary. But, one major mistake we often make is to think, or speak, about the will of God only in connection with certain decisions or when adversity comes. Jesus spoke of his life purpose as doing the will of the Father; and, he further defined that purpose with reference to us as, "to seek and to save the lost," (Luke 19:10) to "give his life as a ransom for many" (Mark 10:45).

It is the will of our heavenly Father that we should be saved. His stories were about a lost sheep, a lost coin, and a lost son. God is like the shepherd who left the ninety-nine sheep and looked for one that was lost. He is like the woman who searched until she found the lost coin. He is like the father who welcomed a returning son, forgave him, and reinstated him in the family. In every case there was rejoicing in heaven when one sinner returned to God (Luke 15).

God does not will the loss of any one of his children. We have confused "election" with "rejection." How strange rejection sounds when we hear Jesus speaking about the little ones whom he loves. While acknowledging the inevitability of temptations which cause these little ones to stumble, Jesus said "but woe to the man by whom temptation comes!" (Matt. 18:7). And then he said, "So it is not the will of my Father who is in heaven that one of these little ones should perish" (Matt. 18:14). God wills our salvation.

Salvation is a relationship with God. It is not something you get; rather, it is a relationship into which you enter. Our obsession with getting things misleads us into misunderstanding salvation. In every instance, it is a returning to God through repentance and faith. In every instance, it results in a reconciliation with God and with others. It is harmony with God resulting in love for God and other persons. That is why Jesus would say, "whoever does the will of my Father in heaven is my brother, and sister, and mother" (Matt. 12:50).

It also follows that when people are right with God, they will do his will. The world is overpopulated with quasi-religious people talking about their religion. Jesus put it simply, not every one who signed up for the course would pass the final examination: "Not every one who says to me, 'Lord, Lord,' shall enter the kingdom of heaven, but he who does the will of my Father who is in heaven" (Matt. 7:21).

Jesus told a story about a man who had two sons. He told them to go and work in the vineyard. One promised to go, but didn't; the other refused, but later changed his mind and went (Matt. 21:28-30). Jesus merely asked, "Which of the two did the will of his father?" (21:31). Even Jesus' critics gave the right answer. Ultimately, rightness with God amounts to a right relationship with God which brings an attitude of obedience in which we just do the will of God. And, "he who does the will of God abides for ever" (1 John 2:17).

## The Will of God and the Unwilling

You raise the question, "But what about those who do not will to do God's will?" We have noted that Jesus knew a struggle between his will and the Father's but he resolved the struggle and obeyed God. We know times in our own experience in which we do not do God's will. But this question has to do with those who choose their own will over God's will permanently.

After Jesus had repeatedly spoken to his contemporaries about God's will and they refused his message, he said, "O Jerusalem, Jerusalem, killing the prophets and stoning those who are sent to you! How often would I have gathered your children together as a hen gathers her brood under her wings, and you would not!" (Matt. 23:37). And you would not!

A rich, alert, upright man came to Jesus asking about eternal life. He had almost everything (or it had him), but he lacked one thing. When Jesus told him to put God first in his life, he went away sorrowful and defeated. His grief was exceeded only by that of Jesus. The man had stood on the threshold, heard about the will of God, but would not. Jesus was grieved at this tragic failure but could not coerce a person into doing God's will. This would have violated both God and man (Matt. 19:16-22).

Our freedom is genuine. We can say no to God. Our distinctive human nature requires this freedom; to be deprived of it for any reason would reduce us to a subhuman existence. God holds us accountable for the use of our freedom. We stand before God who made us. The entire biblical witness points to this wonderful and awesome freedom. But, the burden is great.

There are two classic ways for denying the ultimate burden of our freedom: (1) with a particular interpretation of the doctrine of election, we blame God for making the choice which determines our destiny, or (2) we find a way to deny this freedom ultimately by a doctrine of universal salvation.

There is a double predestinarian view which advocates the notion that God chose those to be saved and those to be lost. If so, then God made the choice for us; we really can do nothing about it. This view appears to be crushed under the burden of biblical teachings calling upon men and women to repent. Such admonitions are meaningless unless people can repent. This view would finally reduce man to a puppet on the end of a string. Not so in the Scripture! God gave us freedom.

The other extreme is universal salvation. Persons with deep appreciation for the love of God reason that God could not accept defeat in the case of one person being lost for eternity. Others reflect on the evils in human history and sin in the lives of all of us. Then, they reason that a God of justice and love could not permit some of us to be lost forever. If, however, all are ultimately to be saved, a person cannot say no to God. If one said no, it would only mean not yet. And, if all are to be saved finally, not yet will eventually mean yes. The teachings of Scripture indicate that we can reject the will of God finally. God does not force his will upon us. We must choose to will what is his will or choose to do our own will.

And you may also be interested in God's will for those parts of creation which have no wills of their own. Time will permit only a brief mention. God sustains all of creation. Jesus spoke of the birds, the lilies, and the grass of the field. Not one sparrow "will fall to the ground without your Father's will" (Matt. 10:29) indicates God's care for all creation although in this statement his point was that persons are of more value than sparrows. There are also statements about creation itself awaiting redemption (Rom. 8:19ff.), but that must wait till later.

Those who do not accept the will of God, or do not know about it, are sustained by the power of God. "He makes his sun rise on the evil and on the good, and sends rain on the just and on the unjust" (Matt. 5:45). Augustine liked to say that God sustains the world at all times and, if he were to stop for a moment, it would fall into the abyss of nothingness. But God's sustaining power is best understood in more personal terms. Paul is a good example.

When Paul was persecuting the church, he was not doing the will of God. When he interrogated these early Christians, however, they witnessed to him about their faith. They were doing the will of God. He was the undeserving and unwitting beneficiary. He held the coats of those who stoned Stephen to death. This was not the will of God. But Stephen in his circumstances prayed for his murderers and witnessed to his faith. This was the will of God.

After Paul's conversion, he could write the Galatians, "But when he who set me apart before I was born, and had called me through his grace" (1:15). Paul certainly did not mean that he was doing God's will when he was persecuting the church. But he does mean that God was working on his behalf even during those incidents. In other words, God's will does affect us sometimes even when we are not aware of it. This can be seen only in retrospect after we have willed to do his will.

### The Will of God and Human Adversity

We have postponed a discussion of God's will in relation to human adversity as long as we can. Jesus was apparently asked questions like those we hear. We will look at three instances: (1) the crime of Pilate in the massacre of the Galileans; (2) the tragic accident in the collapse of the tower of Siloam; and (3) the case of congenital blindness.

Pontius Pilate was guilty of numerous atrocities. Apparently, one had happened not too long before, if not during, Jesus' ministry. Pilate had massacred a group of Galileans at worship and had mingled their blood with that of their sacrifices (Luke 13:1-4). Evidently, some of Jesus' listeners thought they had died because of the judgment of God on their sins. The age-old assumption was that adversity indicated the disfavor of God. Jesus rejected this interpretation. He gave a clear no to this popular assumption.

Jesus pointed out the need for repentance because all face adversity of one kind or another. He refused to speculate on the question they had raised. It was a crime of a wicked man. It was unjust. We must not read into these events some hidden will of God. If we do so, we make God an accomplice, if not the perpetrator, of crimes for which we would send human beings to prison. We can make some explanation about a crime, but that does not deal with the question, "Why us?" or "Why now?" or "Why my loved ones?" Jesus was silent on these questions.

In the same setting, Jesus was asked about the tragic accident when the tower of Siloam fell and killed eighteen persons (Luke 13:4-5). The popular interpretation was the same; these people were notorious sinners and were getting what they deserved. Jesus rejected the interpretation. He called people to repentance.

Many people raise the same question today when accidents happen; and many offer the same interpretation, judgment on sin. We cannot do this. The tower may have collapsed because of shoddy materials or workmanship, but we don't know that. And if we did, that explanation would not answer the question as to why it fell when it did or on those who were killed. In my city, the roof on an arena collapsed. Fortunately, it was not during a sporting event when crowds would have been present. Officials went to work to determine the cause; as well they should. But we are dealing with a different kind of question.

The case of the man born blind is the third illustration of Jesus. I hesitate to discuss this since most of us are closely acquainted with families in which there is such a handicap, injury, illness, or congenital defect. My hesitation is increased because some Christians have interpreted these burdens as God's blessings in disguise. I am hesitant about that interpretation.

The man was born blind. The disciples asked Jesus, "Rabbi, who sinned, this man or his parents, that he was born blind?" (John 9:2). They asked the wrong question; and, they asked it incorrectly. Even Jesus had trouble trying to give the right answer to a wrong question.

The disciples saw only two alternatives. It is unpleasant to be asked a question which spells out the alternatives. They really thought: (1) the unborn infant had sinned in his mother's womb and was being punished; or, (2) the parents had sinned and the child was being punished. The basic error was the assumption that all human suffering was the direct result of human sin. We don't know the villain who concocted the theory that an unborn child could sin and incur blindness before he ever sees. We can trace the erroneous interpretation which has been the basis and perpetuation of the idea of inherited guilt for sin.

Jesus rejected both popular interpretations and, again, spoke of this as an opportunity. He healed the man. This does not mean that God willed the blindness; that would be a more difficult problem than the one facing us. Jesus did not explain or speculate. He responded to the opportunity. This was the will of God for him—to do what he could for the persons in whatever situation he found them. Yes!

The doctrine of original sin is often understood to teach biological transmission of sin and its consequences. But, this is not the intent of the psalmist when he said, "in sin did my mother conceive me" (51:5). He was confessing his own sin—not his mother's. He meant that all of life, even from the moment it began, had been tarnished by sin. Paul was not teaching biological transmission of sin and its consequences in Romans (5:12). Rather, he was contrasting the age of Adam with its sin and death to the age of Christ with grace and life—life eternal. We are sinners because "all men sinned" (Rom. 5:12), and we will be saved when we will to follow Christ. Neither sin nor salvation is inherited.

It seems incredible that people still want to interpret the judgment of God on parents' sins in the lives of their offspring. This had been widely believed in the early Old Testament period, but was under attack by the time of Jeremiah and Ezekiel. Jeremiah quoted the old proverb about the parents having eaten sour grapes and the children's teeth having been set on edge (Jer. 31:29 f.). Ezekiel went further; he indicated that the old interpretation was now forbidden.

The word of the Lord came to me again: "What do you mean by repeating this proverb concerning the land of Israel, 'The fathers have eaten sour grapes, and the children's teeth are set on edge?' As I live, says the Lord God, this proverb shall no more be used by you in Israel . . . the soul that sins shall die'' (Ezek. 18:1-4).

That is, each person is responsible for his or her own sin.

The assumption back of the disciples' question, "Who sinned?" is one of the most sinister threats we meet in trying to understand the will of God. When tragedy comes, it is better to say that we don't know than to guess and thereby multiply both our grief and the injustice. We don't know "Why," or "Why now?" or "Why us?" But we can ask what God would have us do now that it has happened.

### Purity of Heart Is to Will One Thing

Jesus warned against divided loyalty (Matt. 6:22 f.). He recommended single-mindedness, one purpose, one overall commitment to God. "Seek first his kingdom and his righteousness" (Matt. 6:33). Life needs one invariable, one fixed point by which all relatives can be guided—a North Star.

The great saints of the ages have learned this single-minded devotion implied in Jesus' words, "Blessed are the pure in heart" (Matt. 5:8). Purity means unmixed, unalloyed, single, not corrupted. Paul learned it and expressed it in the phrase "one thing I do" (Phil. 3:13). No one in modern times has seen it more clearly than Soren Kierkegaard.

Kierkegaard wrote a little book entitled *Purity of Heart Is to Will One Thing.* He analyzed the teachings of Jesus and the Christian life and concluded that "purity of heart" happens when Christians handle all competing claims and can "will one thing." Jesus believed that purity of heart was to know and do the will of the Father. This commitment will purify us and lead to purity of heart.

"Thy will be done on earth in my life as it is in heaven!"

# 3
# Paul—
# Called by the Will of God

*Paul, called by the will of God to be an apostle of Christ Jesus, and our brother Sosthenes, to the church of God which is at Corinth, to those sanctified in Christ Jesus, called to be saints together with all those who in every place call on the name of our Lord Jesus Christ, both their Lord and ours: Grace to you and peace from God our Father and the Lord Jesus Christ (1 Cor. 1:1-3).*

The expression, "called by the will of God" is unusual, but four other letters bearing Paul's name employ the same terminology (2 Cor. 1:1; Eph. 1:1; Col. 1:1; 2 Tim. 1:1). And in Romans the wording is, a "servant of Jesus Christ, called to be an apostle, set apart for the gospel of God" (Rom. 1:1). In 1 Timothy, it is the "command of God" (1:1) instead of the will of God. The expression states two very important themes: the call and the will of God.

We are concerned at the moment with understanding Paul's teaching on the will of God. Paul understood the will of God to have been made known to him in his call and then as unfolding during his life as an itinerant Christian apostle. Time will not permit a full study of his call or his interpretation of the Christian faith, but we shall try to be faithful to the whole. I have chosen to deal only with the following themes related to the call and will of God: (1) the will of God as the call to an individual; (2) the will of God as a call to the church; (3) the will of God and one's life calling; (4) the will of God as it relates to our salvation; (5) doing the will of God when all is right; (6) doing the will of God when doors lock us out; (7) the will of God in the face of unexplained suffering; and (8) how do we do the will of God when the doors lock us in.

Let us postpone discussion of two very important passages in

Romans (8:28 and 12:1-2) until later chapters.

## An Individual's Call

Paul's call experience was of the utmost importance to him and, because of its presence in the New Testament, to the Christian faith. Paul wrote of it in detail in his letter to the Galatians and alluded to it in other letters. Luke reported it three times in Acts: in narrative form in Acts 9; in Paul's address in the Temple area in Jerusalem (Acts 22); and in Paul's defense before King Agrippa (Acts 26).

The dramatic nature of Paul's call is striking. It was dramatic because of Paul's particular situation as leader of the opposition and because of the radical reversal resulting in his life. This call has been accepted as a model by many Christians who had previously lived rather zealously in another faith or in contradiction to Christian faith. To them it becomes normative. But, we should not make it normative in our understanding of "calling." Many people have responded to the call of God with the same commitment as Paul did but without the dramatic light, voice, and radical reversal. Many of those who have enjoyed growing up in Christian homes have made their decisions of faith in very calm circumstances; they do not recall a radical reversal because they had not previously lived in radical opposition as Paul had.

The essentials of the call were: God took the initiative; the Word of God was proclaimed; the Christian witnesses bore their testimony; the Holy Spirit worked within Paul; Paul responded to God by faith; and, reconciliation resulted.

Paul's call experience appeared to be a direct encounter with God. This is in keeping with Jesus' statement to Peter. Jesus responded to Peter's confession by saying, "For flesh and blood has not revealed this to you, but my Father who is in heaven" (Matt. 16:17). Peter had observed Christ's works and had heard him teach, but the confession of faith happened only when God had worked in Peter. In other words, the confession of faith was not merely the expression of an opinion or even a conclusion. It included all of the evidence, but it was an encounter with God on a deeper level than mere understanding of information.

We must not speculate about Paul's conversion. But, we know from the Scriptures that he had persecuted and interrogated the Christians. They had told him the information about Jesus, the content of the gospel. We need to remember that the Holy Spirit assists those who witness to Christ under such interrogation. Paul also brought with him an intensive knowledge about God from his Old Testament studies and religious tradition. Paul certainly knew his opposition when he angrily departed for Damascus.

The vision of the risen Lord brought his beliefs and doubts into clear focus. Jesus had been raised from the dead as the Christians had said; they were correct; Saul was wrong. He stood in the presence of the Lord; God had made the revelation. Saul responded, "What shall I do, Lord?" Paul always remembered that sacred moment in which the God of all creation had appeared to him and made his will known. Thereafter, Paul gave his life to the doing of God's will as revealed to him.

Faith is this personal, all-inclusive response to God. It is preceded by information about God and belief; but, it is faith only when it reaches the level of personal trust. This kind of trust gives birth to loyalty.

Paul combined his call to be a Christian with his call to be an apostle, or he did not separate the two in his telling. He compressed the will of God into a comprehensive purpose for his whole life. The basic meaning of that call is the primary call of God to faith, as we shall see when Paul spoke to the church. We can learn from Paul and speak of our own individual calling to be Christians. It happens the same way. We hear the gospel; God's witnesses add their testimony; God's Spirit convicts us; we respond by faith; and, we also are reconciled to God. Each one of us has been called!

### The Call and the Church

The call also applies to all Christians together in the church. We experience the call individually as did Paul; but, we immediately become aware that what has happened involves a community of believing persons. Paul heard the gospel in that community, from that community, and became a part of that community just as soon as he had been called. After stressing that he had been "called by the will of God," Paul addressed the church in Corinth as those "called to be saints together with all those who in every place call on the name of our Lord Jesus Christ" (1 Cor. 1:1-3). This greeting was natural for Paul who wrote the Romans, "To all God's beloved in Rome, who are called to be saints" (1:7), and the Galatian Christians who also had been called (Gal. 1:6).

Paul's call to be a Christian was the same as that of all the Christians who are called to be saints. They, too, are dedicated to God. We differ in that we have different gifts which we exercise like members of a body (1 Cor. 12:12-30). Christ gives us unity.

The Christian calling cannot be understood except in terms of the Christian community. Even the most individualistic, and Paul appears at times to have been this way, find their own identity and life only in relation to the others. After the Damascus Road experience, Paul was identified with the Christians in Damascus through the ministry of Ananias. Later he visited the Christians in Jerusalem. He came fully into his own ministry only when he became a part of the Christian community in Antioch. This should indicate to us the vital role of the church when we seek to know and do the will of God. The tension between the individual and the community is creative tension. We serve God, do his will, only as committed individual persons functioning in the family of God, the church. The will of God involves the community.

Paul understood the will of God in his calling to set him apart for an itinerant ministry to the Gentiles. But the other Christians were just as "called" as he was. God's will for them was just as specific and important to them. They were "saints," "dedicated," called according to the will of God. There are no ordinary Christians. We all respond to God's call by faith.

## Paul's Life Calling

Paul identified himself as the apostle to the Gentiles. It was the will of God that he be that apostle. God's purpose for him was that ministry. This calling became the dominant purpose of his life.

Meaningful purpose integrates human life and makes it a power-ful force. An urgency grows in the life that knows such a commit-ment. Paul, for instance, had been entrusted with the mission of proclaiming the gospel. He said, "Woe to me if I do not preach the gospel!" (1 Cor. 9:16). He was not cringing in fear of some punish-ment God might inflict on him if he failed; rather, he was thinking about his own inner condemnation if he failed in so glorious a task. He could find the courage to stand up to the enemy, the traitor, the jailers, the weak governors, the storms at sea, and the beasts in Ephesus; he cringed at the prospect of being unfaithful to Christ. The will of God gave him purpose and motivation. He feared, "lest after preaching to others I myself should be disqualified" (1 Cor. 9:27).

Paul's occupation was making tents. His calling was to be the apostle to the Gentiles. There is a tendency for Christian people to think of God's will in every aspect of their lives. Many handbooks on the will of God deal specifically with choosing a life occupation, choosing a marriage partner, and the like. Certainly, a Christian should pray and seek guidance in all of life's decisions. But, it may be that God gives us more freedom in these areas than we think. Paul was not called to be a tentmaker; he was called to be a Chris-tian minister.

A young engineer in a small town in the Eastern United States was confronted by the challenge of numerous young people in his community needing and seeking guidance. He experienced a renew-ing of faith in his own life and believed God had called him to lead these youth. He had trained as an engineer; his professional assign-ment had brought him to this community. He declined a transfer in order to continue his ministry. He referred to his "calling" to min-ister to these young people while he earned his living as an engineer. This expresses the heart of the Christian life as calling.

The calling to ministry does not usually mean going away to theological school to become a pastor or missionary. For some persons, it does mean that. But, for most persons, it means serving God by ministering in the setting of the call or wherever one might be. Many young persons have misinterpreted this call. They have gone to seminary thinking that was the only way to respond to a call, later learning that they had not been called to a full-time-salaried type of ministry. With considerable difficulty, they reinterpret their calling and work back to their place in their own church community.

The calling is always for full-time ministry whether one is a teacher in the church, a missionary, or serves in other ways. The matter of receiving a salary has nothing to do with the call to ministry. Obviously, pastors and missionaries and many other ministers must have a professional education to be qualified for their ministries. But, other ministers must also have their qualifications. It is, of course, reasonable for churches to pay salaries to its ministers who give all of their time in the ministry; it is necessary to do so in order to get visas for missionaries to foreign countries. But, calling has nothing to do with that. Paul made tents. And, most ministers today have occupations and professions in which they earn their livelihood. Those of us who devote full time to a particular ministry and receive salaries for so doing could find ways of earning our livelihood if it were necessary in order to continue our ministry. At any rate, all Christians are called to serve Christ. And, the will of God does not necessarily designate one's occupation.

However, when devoted Christians know and speak about God's will for their lives, it usually is comprehensive. People relate all of life to God's will. Head coach Tom Landry of the Dallas Cowboys was quoted in a newspaper article as saying: "I don't look back on what I've done. I know this sounds foolish to many people, perhaps ridiculous to non-Christians, but I believe it was God's will that I be what I am—a coach . . . . With this in mind, I have no hangups at all about what I might have done or been."[1] Tom Landry's reputation as a Christian gentleman and a committed disciple is almost as well-known as his reputation in football. You will note his awareness that non-Christians might think his language strange. But, he was right that a Christian would understand. He is a very successful coach. You may be a schoolteacher, carpenter, electrician, or athlete. The point is that a person who is genuinely committed to Christ, whatever his way of earning a living, finds a ministry in his setting which integrates the rest of life. And, we can say, "I am where God wants me"; or "It is God's will that I be here doing what I am doing."

## Salvation

Paul, like Jesus before him, related our salvation to the will of God. The word *salvation* is a broad one. Salvation includes the beginning—often spoken of as conversion, new birth, new creation, or atonement. Also included is the continuation of salvation, often spoken of as sanctification. Finally, the idea of assurance, or our confidence of our relationship with God is a part of salvation. Paul spoke of all three aspects in terms of the will of God.

Christ's saving work, or atoning work, on our behalf was done according to the will of God. In one of the earliest letters, Paul wrote that the Lord Jesus Christ "gave himself for our sins to deliver us from the present evil age, according to the will of our God and Father" (Gal. 1:4). And, "while we were enemies we were reconciled to God by the death of his Son" (Rom. 5:10). Also, he "destined us in love to be his sons through Jesus Christ, according to the purpose of his will" (Eph. 1:5).

Christ's atoning work, our reconciliation to God, was not an afterthought with God. God had worked toward this event throughout history and sent Christ in the fullness of time (Gal. 4:4-6). Christ "died for our sins in accordance with the scriptures" (1 Cor. 15:3).

Sanctification is that continuous work of grace which God accomplishes within us. It is a process in which God reclaims all of our lives from sin. "This is the will of God, your sanctification," Paul wrote the Thessalonians (1 Thess. 4:3). Instruction for growth in the Christian virtues is a part of the process, and it, too, is identified as the will of God for us: "Rejoice always, pray constantly, give thanks in all circumstances; for this is the will of God in Christ Jesus for you" (1 Thess. 5:16-18).

So the will of God for us as Christians places a heavy emphasis on our growth into full maturity as committed persons. The will of God is not a mysterious riddle to be solved; it is the redemptive purpose of God that each of us continue to grow in personal salvation, both individually and collectively. God wills it and works within us and on our behalf toward that goal. Note the promise: "We know that in everything God works for good with those who love him" (Rom. 8:28). But he expects diligent work on our part: "Work out your own salvation with fear and trembling; for God is at work in you, both to will and to work for his good pleasure" (Phil. 2:12-13). "Good pleasure" is God's will. Furthermore, believers are urged to "understand what the will of the Lord is" (Eph. 5:17).

People ask, "Can we know that we are right with God?" or "How can we know that we are saved?" The word *know* is not used in the sense of mathematical proof; the word means confidence, personal conviction, assurance.

Paul suggested the Spirit's presence as a test for assurance: "the Spirit himself bearing witness with our spirit that we are the children of God" (Rom. 8:16). John proposed the test of love: "We know that we have passed out of death into life, because we love the brethren" (1 John 3:14). Paul believed that it is the will of God that we have assurance of our relationship with God. Paul reminded the Colossians, "that you may stand mature and fully assured in all the will of God" (4:12).

It is the will of God that men and women shall know the full meaning of New Testament salvation, reconciliation with God, and that they shall have confidence about it.

## When All Goes Well

Paul worked out his missionary journeys like he worked out his missionary theology, while he traveled. Paul wrote his letters, and hence recorded his theological reflections, in response to specific human situations. In the same way, he planned his missionary itinerary. In so doing, he sought to know the will of God and to interpret it in the light of problems and challenges as they arose in daily life. Lystra, Iconium, Antioch, Jerusalem, Caesarea, a shipwreck in the Mediterranean, a jail in Philippi, a synagogue in Corinth, and a prison in Rome provided the setting and some of the insight for understanding the will of God as it related to him and his ministry.

The apostle loved preaching the gospel. He was an itinerant preacher; his parish was the Roman Empire. He was confident God had called him to the task. The church in Antioch had been led by the Holy Spirit and Barnabas to stand with Paul and his missionary companions. Men like Barnabas, Silas, Timothy, and Luke shared the calling with him. When they preached in a city, a small congregation formed in response to this word of God. This community would carry on the work which Paul and the others had begun. Paul could then go on to new areas. The will of God for him became clearer as he and his companions journeyed. The involvement of the church of Antioch and the others along the way added to Paul's conviction that this was God's will. In spite of frequent opposition, clearly God participated in their task. And, in that setting Paul learned more about the will of God, while doing that which he loved most of all.

Doing the will of God does not remove the need for making and following plans. Paul had a number of purely human principles which he followed in his missionary work. He worked in major cities and cities of commerce from which the gospel could spread to the surrounding regions. He followed a strategy of not working in cities in which other missionaries had already planted Christian churches. He earned his living making tents, thinking it best not to receive a salary from these communities, but he encouraged them to give to worthy causes such as to relieve poverty in Jerusalem. He maintained a rather close relationship with the churches in Antioch and Jerusalem, as well as the churches spread out over the Graeco-Roman world. Even when he was in jail, he sent and received letters from these congregations. Doing the will of God does not alleviate the need for sound planning. Paul evidently believed that God in his own way leads human beings as they make and work their plans.

Paul planned his missionary work with a geographical goal in mind. He wanted to establish churches westward from Jerusalem in

Judea, and Antioch in Syria, through Asia Minor, and finally to Rome, the center of the empire, and on to Spain. It is very interesting to note that while he made his plans to do what he enjoyed doing, he acknowledged a leadership from God which could permit or prevent his doing the plans. He wrote the Roman Christians that he had prayed for them, "asking that somehow by God's will I may now at last succeed in coming to you" (Rom. 1:10). He worked his plan in most instances.

Near the end of the Roman letter, Paul gave a clear picture of his own planning and his recognition of God's will as it was involved. He had followed his plan from Jerusalem to Illyricum. He had Spain in his plan. Others had preached in Rome before he arrived, but he wanted the Roman church to participate in the mission to Spain and planned to convince them on his visit *en route* (Rom. 15:19-24). But when he wrote the letter to Rome, he was bound for Jerusalem, in the opposite direction, to deliver the money which the Macedonian Christians had given for the poor in Jerusalem. He had made a commitment to these Christians; it took priority over his other plans for the moment (15:28).

A note of anxiety emerged in Paul's letter in which he otherwise spoke with such enthusiasm about his plans. He planned to go to Jerusalem and deliver the gift and his obligation, then Rome, and on to Spain. But Paul had learned that God did not guarantee the plans even for the apostle to the Gentiles. Paul feared trouble in Jerusalem which might change or terminate all of his plans. He expressed the hope that he would "be delivered from the unbelievers in Judea" (15:31). God's will in matters like missionary plans does not mean a "fixed plan." In some way, it takes into account a changing human situation. But while all of his plans could have been ended in a single rash act in Jerusalem, Paul asked the friends in Rome, whom he had never met, to pray "that by God's will I may come to you with joy and be refreshed in your company" (15:32).

Paul suffered from anxieties and uncertainties, such as we face. He made his plans, prayed, and went on when he could. He loved to preach. He loved to travel. Rome drew him like a magnet. In spite of the uncertainties and dangers, the apostle to the Gentiles found doing the will of God sheer fun.

## When Doors Lock Us Out

Henry and Helen Turlington went to China as missionaries in the late 1940s. They believed they were doing the will of God. The Communist takeover in that country forced them to leave. They spent most of their ministry in the States where Dr. Turlington was a professor and a pastor. Then, in the seventies there was an opportunity for another attempt at overseas missions. They were appointed to Tehran, Iran. After about two years, they were forced to leave Iran. Since Iran is closed to them, they are going to India. What about the will of God when plans fail and doors close locking us out?

The early mission movement was disrupted by a clash over one member of the team. John Mark left the mission in Pamphylia, an act which Paul considered desertion in the face of the enemy. Barnabas wanted to give Mark another chance, but Paul would not. Sharp contention led to a separation of the group (Acts 15:39). Plans failed; there was a personal failure; Mark was locked out of one grand opportunity. He had to take another opportunity. It is to Paul's credit that he later forgave Mark and was reconciled to him and even expressed appreciation for him (Col. 4:10).

The missionary group composed of Paul, Silas, and Timothy was forbidden to enter Bithynia as planned. We don't know what prevented their entry, but the doors were closed and they were in Troas regrouping (Acts 16:6). They did not know the will of God, but when an opportunity came in the form of an invitation to Macedonia, they went. Paul interpreted the invitation to be the will of God: "God had called us to preach the gospel to them" (Acts 16:10).

When doors lock us out, we look for and enter open doors which lead to opportunities for us to carry on our tasks. Paul thought this was one way in which God made his will known to his followers. It allows both for human responsibility and divine guidance. It also allows us room for interpretations of God's will which may or may not be completely just in all implications. For instance, people casually say, "God closed the door." Perhaps he did, or perhaps someone else did. The point to be stressed is that God has an open door or leads us even when doors close. Paul's strife with Barnabas over Mark led to division. There are those who like to point out that this was God's way of organizing a new mission team—two teams instead of one. People who fight and divide churches often interpret later that it was God's will. They say, "God works in a mysterious way, his wonders to perform." One can build a rather strong case against some of these interpretations. In some cases, the persons involved are claiming a role for God in the division which was in fact solely filled by contentious persons. It is very unlikely that God has much to do with the contentions which usually divide churches. It is an evidence of his grace that he does not abandon either group but forgives them and helps them go on. Then, in a sense of fair play, let us not blame God for our contentious spirit. Rather, let us thank him for his grace.

## Unexplained Suffering

One of the most serious questions raised about the will of God has to do with human suffering. A young man loses his eyesight while seeking to do God's will. A young woman who has committed her life to a Christian calling is injured in an accident and goes through life in a wheelchair. They ask, "Is this the will of God?"

Paul had a "thorn" in his side which in his judgment was a severe handicap hindering his missionary work. He prayed to God repeatedly for its removal, but God did not remove it. Paul had to go on suffering. How many people do we all know who spend so much of their lives suffering from some malady? These people often express resentment toward God for such senseless suffering. And, many of them do not find a way to go on as Paul did. What about the will of God with reference to this suffering?

There are numerous speculations as to what Paul's "thorn" was: persecution; temptations of the flesh; spiritual trials, such as times of doubt or depression; some physical malady such as epilepsy, eye disease, or nervous disorder. We just don't know. The most likely guesses would include some kind of physical malady like seizures or debilitating illness. Paul spoke of his own embarrassment and suggested that he may have been offensive to his hosts (Gal. 4:13-15). Of course, that reference may have had nothing to do with the "thorn." At any rate, it was a kind of suffering that was also a hindrance to his work.

There was no cure for the malady; instead, there was an assurance of victory over it, "My grace is sufficient for you, for my power is made perfect in weakness" (2 Cor. 12:7-9). Paul spoke on several occasions of his tendency to boast. This "thorn" humbled him. In retrospect, he saw that it served one corrective purpose in his life. His "thorn" encouraged humility. But, he did not say that "God willed it"; rather, he identified it as a "messenger of Satan, to harass me" (2 Cor. 12:7). Paul was a very courageous and "faithful" person. He could go on without a cure or an explanation. He continued on the basis of God's adequate grace. And, of course, it would be ideal if we could follow his lead. But I am often told that we simply are not as strong as Paul and that this is not enough for us.

The irrational nature of much suffering places us in a helpless position when asked to give a rational explanation or justification of it. The question is usually worded, If God is good and powerful, why this evil? The implication is that he either does not want to remove evil or lacks the power to do so. If we hold to the idea that God is loving and powerful, we must go to some rationale, such as God permits evil and suffering for some greater good or even is responsible for sending evil and suffering for a good purpose. We derive some help from the awareness that much suffering appears to result from human sin, either personal or collective, and its accumulated effect in human experience. But, we are still left with a rational problem which will not yield to an easy solution. Later, we shall talk about a kind of suffering which is redemptive. This will help. But, a serious problem remains.

## When Doors Lock Us In

Dietrich Bonhoeffer was executed in prison in April of 1945 while liberating armies swept twoard the prison in which he had spent nearly two years. Although he was only thirty-nine years of age, he had made a remarkable impact on theology and church life in Europe. He had been one of the churchmen who recognized quite early the depth of Hitler's evil design and had resisted. He is a hero today for many younger church leaders. While in prison, deprived of his parish and classroom, he continued to be a minister, caring for others and giving comfort. He wrote his famous *Letters from Prison*, fragments of which survive. They tell of his vibrant and insightful faith; they reflect no terror or self-pity. Although he was locked in, he found a way to live with God, minister to others. And he got some word to the outside world, even while in a Nazi prison.

Bonhoeffer's actions in the 1930s stir admiration in many. He had insight and courage. But others regarded him as a traitor. He went to Sweden early in the war, met with British churchmen to discuss a plan in Germany to overthrow Hitler, and sought their help in swaying England and America to end the war by negotiation. He was privy to the plot to assassinate Hitler. Most governments regard such activity as treason. Without going further with Bonhoeffer, let me only say that knowing and doing the will of God in a world like Bonhoeffer's was not a simple task. It is not a simple task in our world. However, even when we are locked up, some windows remain open through which we can continue to do the will of God, at least in a limited way.

In Jerusalem, Paul's status as missionary was changed to that of prisoner. But Paul did not change. He went to Rome, not as he had planned; he went in chains, but he went. We cannot be certain that he wrote the letter to Philippi from the jail in Rome, but this interpretation enjoys traditional acceptance. In that prison, at least before he was condemned, he received his missionary messengers, sent his letters, and carried on his business. It was not "business as usual," but he did not close down his missionary enterprise. He took advantage of his opportunities to evangelize his guards and wrote, "what has happened to me has really served to advance the gospel" (Phil. 1:12). It was not an ideal missionary headquarters, but Paul found a way to operate from prison, when doors locked him in.

Slavery appears in a passage about the will of God. In Ephesus, slaves and masters had evidently come into the church. The admonition does not condone slavery; neither does it condemn it. "Slaves, be obedient to those who are your earthly masters, with fear and trembling, in singleness of heart, as to Christ; . . . . as servants of Christ, doing the will of God from the heart" (Eph. 6:5-6). Masters were likewise instructed. The story of Philemon and Onesimus illustrates the social dilemma which confronted the early church.

Many modern interpreters are disappointed in Paul for not taking a stand against slavery. It can be said only that Paul spoke for the redemption of the persons caught on both sides of an evil human practice. It was the will of God for both slave and master to live toward the other with personal love and Christian understanding. We could point out that slavery did eventually fall before a Christian spirit. Some would say that it is a position difficult to maintain, however, since Christians and many churches have been exceedingly slow to accept, let alone bring about, the full implications of human equality.

We don't approve of slavery in the first Christian century or any other. And we don't approve the injustice which is perpetrated by governments, political parties, large economic corporations, labor unions, ecclesiastical bodies, and other human collectives. But can we see that God has a will for the persons caught in such locked-door situations? Can we see that such a will focuses on the persons and their welfare until such time as the injustices can be removed and the situations changed?

Leslie Weatherhead speaks of this as the "circumstantial will" of

God. He contrasts it with the "ultimate will" of God which, of course, forbids slavery. However, the only will of God we know anything about comes in a set of "circumstances." Even the "ultimate will" is known to us only in human circumstances. Can we seek to know the will of God in our circumstances? If so, how do we recognize it?

The letter called 2 Timothy was written from prison. Paul spoke as an old man, worn and scarred from numerous engagements, nearing the end of one journey. He wrote to a younger missionary, Timothy:

For I am already on the point of being sacrificed; the time of my departure has come. I have fought the good fight, I have finished the race, I have kept the faith. Henceforth there is laid up for me the crown of righteousness, which the Lord, the righteous judge, will award to me on that Day, and not only to me but also to all who have loved his appearing (2 Tim. 4:6-8).

What courage! Paul was about to start off on another journey. He would not report back to Antioch or Jerusalem this time but to God who had called him by his will to be an apostle. "Called by the will of God" to the very last!

What Paul could have said is contained in a text from his wisdom studies, "A man's mind plans his way, but the Lord directs his steps" (Prov. 16:9)!

# 4
# A Preview—
# The Guiding Stars

Let us continue our discussion of doing the will of God by comparing it with making a journey. The sailors of earlier days depended on the stars and constellations to guide them across the sea. What are the major stars and constellations which promise to guide us as we seek to know and do the will of God?

## The Christian View of God

We are convinced that God the Creator has revealed himself most clearly in Jesus Christ. While he is sovereign of the whole universe, he is the Father of our Lord Jesus Christ. Without familiarity and with reverence, we address him as heavenly Father and believe that he lives with and within us as the Holy Spirit.

God is loving and caring. He wills for us lives of meaning and worth. If we know how to give good gifts to our children, how much more does our heavenly Father desire to give us lives that are rich and pure. We speak of the will of God in terms of this understanding of God.

Inasmuch as he revealed himself most clearly in Jesus Christ, we look to Christ for our beliefs about God. We understand the will of God in the light of Jesus' disclosure and teaching.

When we depart from the basic view of God as revealed in Christ, for whatever reason and however good our intentions may be, we distort our understanding of the will of God. Our most common error is exaggerating the truth in one area and neglecting it in the others. For instance, we may dwell on the sovereignty of God and forget God's personal nature. If we do it to the extreme, we can depersonalize or objectify God. It does not take long to go into idolatry this way. That particular view of God tends to see the will of God as a fixed fatalistic plan instead of the "good pleasure" of the heavenly Father.

When God created human beings and gave us "dominion," he imposed a limit, even though temporary, upon himself. This self-limitation of God seems to be the only way he could give us a genuine existence in freedom. This, of course, means that God delegated power to us. In misusing our freedom and power, we sinned against God and all other creatures. Much of the evil, if not all of it, which we encounter should be charged to human beings rather than to God. Evil may exist in a larger sense than human sin in its terrifying global manifestation, but sin is our basic evil. Evil does not have its origin in God, but in the human rejection of God. Correct thinking about God is our first navigational star in seeking the will of God.

## A Christian View of Human Life

We believe that God created men and women in his own image. This suggests several possible interpretations: it may designate our dominion over the rest of creation; it may designate our relationship with God; it may speak of our destiny as God's children.

Human beings stand apart from the rest of creation because of their particular relationship with God. We are under God and over nature. We are in nature, but transcend it. We exercise a kind of sovereignty under God's total sovereignty. He delegated this power to us; he can withdraw it whenever he wishes. So long as we are men and women in this world, we exercise power in this "in-between" role. We have wills, and we decide and act in freedom. Our actions have consequences.

Our existence demonstrates the twin characteristics of freedom and responsibility. Our freedom includes the ability to make choices. But, our freedom goes beyond making choices to continuous living and developing character. We may misuse our freedom; we can even turn against God. We can say no to God. This does not mean that God's ultimate purpose in creation will be defeated, but it may well mean that our part of it could be an ultimate loss.

We are responsible. We must respond to God and the world

around us. We must respond to the persons with whom we share the planet. We must give an account to God. We must also be accountable to others and even to those unborn generations.

We sinned against God and in so doing we lost our relationship, purpose, and way. Salvation restores us to God and puts us back on the way. We cannot understand our own human existence apart from this tragic event of our own sin. The major theme of Scripture is God's work of redeeming us from that sin.

If our view of human existence is correct, then we must always discuss our lives from the standpoint of God's purpose or expectation for us—his will. We could never think of our freedom as to "do as we please." We think, rather, of the purpose of God who created us. That is God's "good pleasure," the will of God.

We are not free then to do according to any whim that may strike us. We are free to live in God's world with his other creatures and according to his purpose. But we are not automatons either. We are not pawns of necessity; God does not force us to do his will. He has given us only two ultimate choices—not three. We must choose whether we will trust him or go against him. There is no neutral third choice.

The freedom promised in the gospel is liberation from the tyranny of sin so that we can now be the creatures God intended us to be. There are two alternatives: We can acknowledge God and joyfully obey him as we achieve our destiny; or, we can remain servants of sin and "fallen" from God. A correct view of human life is essential for those who would do the will of God.

## A Christian View of Salvation

From an individual standpoint, salvation is restoration to God through repentance and faith and is followed by joyful worship and obedience. Salvation is not something one gets, but it is a relationship into which one enters and continues to abide. The whole meaning of forgiveness of sins is the removal of the barrier which stood between us and God and the reconciliation of the estranged parties. Reconciliation marks the beginning and continuation of Christian life lived under God's guidance, for God's purpose in the world.

Salvation is not merely individual; it is always in relationship to other persons. Sin is not just individual; it is also corporate. Indeed, we are all sinners individually; but we are also tied up together as sinners in the human family. Likewise, salvation is both individual and corporate.

Reconciliation to God means reconciliation to other persons. It involves a living relationship in God's family. Only in that family can we be restored. Selfishness was a large part, if not the primary element, of our sin. Salvation is away from self-centeredness. It is in this way that we are truly transformed into God's image. That is why we must learn to pray "not my will, but thy will." "Thy will" catches up in itself all those other wills and reconciles us to them.

It is appropriate for us to speak of God's call to us to be saved and to do his will. When we hear the voice of God speaking through the gospel, the Holy Spirit, and the witness of others, we can understand it as a call from God.

But salvation may go beyond our individual and collective experience of it to include all of creation. Even if we don't know how to speak of that clearly, we can live in a hope or expectation so as to participate in this fullness of God's restoration of creation. We can do the will of God much better if we have a correct understanding of salvation.

## The Christian View of Providence

Christians believe that God who created the world maintains a sovereignty over it in terms of sustaining and governing creation. He has endowed creation with an orderliness upon which we depend. But Christians have never been able to view the world as the Deists did. We think of God in a continuing relationship. Hence, we think of God's personal involvement in history and in human life.

We often do not see how God may be working in history or nature. We see in retrospect what we believe to have been God's working in both nature and history.

On occasions we think God works within human beings, as in the case of Joseph. The wise and forgiving person who suffered a wrong at the hands of others is able to mediate God's saving forgiveness to those who did the wrong. Redemptive suffering appears to be one way God works.

We believe that God actively works together with us for good in all things, even within things that otherwise appear to be evil. This promise is a foundation for hope in the future and even in adversity. One cannot live in the will of God unless that person cherishes God's providence.

### Christian Hope

The Old Testament faith stressed a promise—what God planned to do within and for his people. The New Testament stresses a fulfillment of that promise in Christ. The New Testament faith became a new and larger hope. We expect Christ's return, the resurrection from the dead, and eternal life with God. We hope in this world that God has great things in store for his creatures. Hope stands with faith and love. Hope is faith looking into the future.

At times Christians have lost sight of their human and earthly hope, despaired of the world, and lived only in hope of another world. This is a tragic confession of unbelief. To be sure, we cherish the eternal hope. On the other hand, we believe God is the Creator of this world, and it is good. We have hope here in this world now.

The pilgrimage we call the Christian life is a journey toward this cherished goal; it is not a flight from some undesirable past. We are pilgrims, not fugitives. We have a joyful expectation of what God has in store for us.

When we seek to know and do the will of God, these stars are in our sky. We look to them when we seek to know his will. They guide us. We hold to a belief that God is our heavenly Father; we are his creatures who individually and as a family live with purpose in his world. God seeks our complete salvation in this life; by his providence he guides and works with us as we do his will. He has given us a joyful and unquenchable hope.

With the guidance of these navigational stars, we live according to God's will.

# 5
# A Promise—
# God Works with Us for Good in All Things

*We know that in everything God works for good with those who love him, who are called according to his purpose (Rom. 8:28).*

Paul started the great eighth chapter of Romans with the proclamation that there is no condemnation for those who "are in Christ Jesus" because they have been set free. He concluded the chapter with the boldest statement of all about assurance: Nothing can separate believers from the love of God in Christ. In between, Paul stressed God's great accomplishment for us through Christ, gave the assurance of the presence of the Spirit with us, and stressed the importance of hope. He then gave the most often quoted statement on promise and providence to be found in the New Testament.

## God and His Promise

The will of God is his purpose for us within the rest of his creation. We should not think of God's will as a finished, detailed plan like the blueprint for a building or a map to be followed in laying a pipeline. Rather, we should think of this purpose in terms of God as he made himself known in Christ and lives with and within us as the Holy Spirit. The promise is God's promise. He has pledged to work actively with those committed to him so that they can do his will.

There are religious views, and they have been known in Christianity, which obscure this working of God. Two examples are Deism and pantheism.

Deism was popular during the early days of United States history. Some of the founders of this country were Deists. Deism designates an outlook on reality which assumes that a God (Deus) created the world; established its laws; and then, for all practical purposes, abandoned it to work of itself. This leads to the belief that the world is something like a huge machine with its controls built-in. This view was popular in the age of emerging theories about natural law. It has some advantages. It is a reasonable conjecture about the origin of the universe; it is consistent with the idea of unity within the universe; it allows the fullest freedom for human potential in the world without any interference by God. It is obvious, however, that Deism left no room or opportunity for God to maintain a meaningful, continuing relationship with the world. For that reason, Christians have rejected Deism. Christians believe that God continues a relationship with his creation. We pray. Deists had no reason to do so.

Pantheism is a view of God and reality which merges the two into one. Somehow God is ever-present, in everything. God permeates all reality. So, the distinction between God and creation is lost. This view has poetic appeal to many, but most Christians have rejected it. The holiness of God forbids the merging. God is holy! We think God remains distinct from his creation but relates to it. We speak of his personal purpose for his creation. His will for us is a personal purpose that our lives shall be and do that which is good in his sight.

### Providence

We discuss God's continuing relationship with his creation under the term *providence*. The term contains at least two elements: governance and sustenance. A third may be required: cooperation and concurrence.

Governance designates the belief that God governs or guides his creation. God delegated dominion and power to his creatures, but he retains his sovereignty over them. Rulers of great kingdoms who exercise tremendous power are called into judgment by God. He remains sovereign. We have looked at some instances in which God so guided persons that his will was accomplished even in evil situations. This is providence as guidance.

Sustenance designates the belief that God sustains the world with his power. The world depends on him. Biblical faith never portrays creation as self-existent; it depends on God. This view is difficult for modern minds, hence the idea of providence is difficult. It is not necessary to reject a scientific view of nature in order to hold to the belief that God sustains creation. The tension between these outlooks requires consideration.

Cooperation designates the belief that God works *with* his creation to achieve his purpose. The word *concurrence* seeks to point out that God can be working concurrently in an event along with persons who are acting and working out of their own motivation and freedom. The promise in Romans 8:28 is this promise of "working together with."

The primary foundation for this belief in concurrence, or providence, is the saving work of Jesus Christ. However, concurrence is also present in the Old Testament. Paul was convinced that God had acted to save sinful people through the life, death, and resurrection of Jesus. God had manifested great power in sending the Holy Spirit in the life of the church. He had demonstrated in the expansion of the young church his continuing presence and power. The text of promise before us states that the activity of God is not limited to occasional and isolated events of great significance. Rather, God works in everything, "for good with those who love him, who are called according to his purpose" (Rom. 8:28).

## A Problem of Two Translations

The ancient manuscripts of the New Testament vary in their presentation of this statement. Some of those manuscripts include the words *ho Theos*, translated "God." Other manuscripts omit those words. The translators following the manuscripts which include *ho Theos* are required to translate something like, "God works together in all things," or "God works all things" or "God works in everything." Translators following the manuscripts which do not include the *ho Theos* may translate it the same way since the verb includes the subject and the context suggests that God is the subject. But the Greek wording allows the "all things" or "everything" to be the subject. When *ho Theos* is missing, the forms of the words allow either translation.

The King James Version, known as the Authorized Version, followed the text which did not include *ho Theos* and translated Romans 8:28, "And we know that all things work together for good to them that love God, to them who are called according to his purpose." No other translation has been so influential in the English speaking world as the King James Version. For this reason, the view that "all things work together for good" has been a prevailing idea.

Representative translations are printed for the sake of comparison.

"And in everything, as we know, he co-operates for good with those who love God and are called according to his purpose" (NEB).

"And we know that to them that love God all things work together for good, even to them that are called according to his purpose" (ASV).

"And we know that God causes all things to work together for good to those who love God, to those who are called according to His purpose" (NASB).

"And we know that in all things God works for the good of those who love him, who have been called according to his purpose" (NIV).

"We know that in all things God works for good with those who love him, those whom he has called according to his purpose" (TEV).

## A Preferred Translation

A preferred translation is the one that makes God the subject and reads "in everything God works for good with . . . ." This translation has sound textual evidence for the reading *ho Theos*. Even if *ho Theos* were not in the text, the tense of the verb allows "God" to be the subject; a subject must be supplied in the translation.

C. H. Dodd argued in his commentary on Romans that the verb form, even when "God" is not in the text, requires the translation to say either "he" or "God."

The translation "in everything God works" is also preferable because it is more consistent with the context in Romans than the other would be. No other New Testament writer, to my knowledge, taught that everything works out for good even for those who love God and are called by him.

A strict interpretation of the translation "all things work together for good" seems much more optimistic than the New Testament generally. It suggests a principle in operation; the other translation points to God cooperating with his people in all things. A rigid view of "all things working together for good" sounds deterministic and tends to diminish the radical evil which otherwise confronts us. Evil is irrational and contradictory; it defies our rational explanations; but it is very serious in biblical faith. It is one thing to say that God can bring good to pass out of evil situations or to say that God works with us for good in evil situations. But it is something quite different to say, "all things work together for good."

Some things do not work out for good. They work out for enduring evil. Some people develop patience and endurance in suffering; others become embittered. Those who do grow stronger through exposure to suffering from the evil deeds of others have resources that need to be identified. God's presence with them is one factor, as are encouragement of other persons at the right time and in the right way and expectations of those who love and care. There are also those who pray and give strength and goodwill. God works through these resources. But there are persons who endure sufferings without those other persons who care, encourage, expect, and pray.

### God's Promise—Cooperation

The beautiful promise of God is that he will work "with us for good" in everything and in every situation. God not only has a will for us but he also works with us to achieve that will. This means that no adversity, whatever its origin or intensity, is beyond the reach of God. We can live in the hope that God will work with us in those extremities to bring about some good in us or for others or both.

God has sustained his people in prisons, persecutions, in the rivers, at the stake, during illnesses, and in humiliation. He promised us that he will work with us in everything we encounter. This is his way of helping us do his will.

Then, after I have gone through the ordeal and have emerged a stronger Christian, I can thank God for his active working with me for good. It may not be right to thank him for the ordeal; someone else may have planned to ruin me in the ordeal and without God's help may have succeeded. It may sound religious to thank God for suffering; I should prefer to thank him for his working with me during suffering. One might be thankful to have had measles because, thereafter, immunity prevents a recurrence. Many illnesses are not that way. They threaten one's very existence. I shall go on thanking God for seeing me through, but I shall not thank him for the illness. At the risk of being ungrateful, I still think another origin is likely.

A young man of sixteen lost his father. Since he was the only son in the family, he assumed a heavy responsibility while a very young man. He had a measure of maturity. Instead of living in resentment or self-pity, he shouldered the burden. It appears that he is carrying it well. If he becomes a much stronger person as a result of this discipline, we shall thank God for his victory. It remains to be seen, however, whether he will suffer later because of the years of youth he has had to skip. And if he is stronger, we shall thank God for his working with the young man, the others who encouraged him and prayed for him, and the gratitude of the other family members who inspired him to perform beyond himself. The loss, the suffering, is the occasion; the causes for his victory will be numerous. The loss is not the cause of his strength; it was the occasion in which it developed.

The verb phrase "work with" or "cooperate" suggests that we are also working for good to achieve the will or "purpose" of God.

It is easy to forget this while enjoying the beautiful promise.

Paul had written the Philippians, "And I am sure that he who began a good work in you will bring it to completion at the day of Jesus Christ" (1:6). Salvation is by grace through faith; we do not achieve salvation by our works. But, those who know Christ's redemption join in the work. So, "work out your own salvation with fear and trembling; for God is at work in you, both to will and to work for his good pleasure" (2:12-13). God promises to work with and within us. "Now to him who by the power at work within us is able to do far more abundantly than all that we ask or think, to him be glory in the church and in Christ Jesus to all generations, for ever and ever. Amen" (Eph. 3:20-21).

The will of God for us includes not only his purpose but also his promise to work with us in achieving it. It is his "good pleasure" that we live our lives in the vertical dimension as well as the horizontal. We can be faithful. We can learn to do right whether or not it is profitable. We are now ready to deal with the question of learning more precisely how we prove what is God's will for us.

# 6
# Proof—
# Proving What Is the Will of God

*I appeal to you therefore, brethren, by the mercies of God, to present your bodies as a living sacrifice, holy and acceptable to God, which is your spiritual worship. Do not be conformed to this world but be transformed by the renewal of your mind, that you may prove what is the will of God, what is good and acceptable and perfect (Rom. 12:1-2).*

When I was a child I heard several sermons on the subject of making excuses. I recall how funny it sounded to me when the minister read the parable of the "Great Supper," and one excuse was "I have bought five yoke of oxen, and I go to prove them: I pray thee have me excused" (Luke 14:19, KJV). I was beginning to learn about a contemporary understanding of "proof" which was different. In our culture, "proof" is more at home in mathematics, geometry, and chemistry. Recent translations use, "I go to examine them" or "am on my way to try them out" (TEV). But in this case the King James Version is better.

A smart ox buyer always "proves" the oxen. Examination is not enough. Where else does one prove oxen except under the yoke, alongside another ox, in tandem with other yokes of oxen, and with a burden behind them? Only then does one know.

When we speak of knowing the will of God, we are speaking of this kind of proving. It has to be under the yoke, alongside others, and with the burden. Do you want to know the will of God? Paul told us how in Romans.

When we speak of knowing the will of God, we are speaking about personal acquaintance and relationship. Having come to believe in him, we pray to him, believe he hears, and responds. We *know* him in faith. This certainly does not imply that we know everything about him. When we say we know the will of God, we mean that we recognize God's purpose for our lives to a degree adequate for us to live for him. We certainly don't mean knowledge in some exhaustive sense. Mystery remains.

This is not the kind of knowledge one acquires from reading the morning newspaper. Paul did not write the Romans to fill in the gaps of information which they lacked. He certainly did not write the letter to satisfy their curiosity. Paul had been transformed by faith in Christ. He had come to know the will of God. The Christians in Rome had also been transformed by faith. They were interested in the will of God as Paul was.

To prove what is the will of God is to learn and affirm in living experience what is "good and acceptable and perfect" in the sight of God. This is the kind of knowledge which, having been affirmed in life, is repeated in testimony, convictions of life, ethical decisions, and later confirmed by the evident fruits of one's labors.

## Knowing God's Will by Faith

We know some things in a purely intellectual sense; we know other things with the total being, existentially, not merely with the intellect. *Faith* is that word which gathers into itself knowledge but moves beyond to trust and commitment. It is the way we "know" God and his will. The author of Hebrews grasped it when he said, "By faith we understand that the world was created by the word of God" (11:3).

God, whom we know, revealed himself in Jesus Christ, thus showing us who he is. He is heavenly Father. God took the initiative in revealing himself. Jesus Christ is the most complete revelation (Col. 1:19), the incarnate Word (John 1:14), God with us redeeming us (2 Cor. 5:19). This reconciliation happens when we, having learned about him and having believed that the gospel is true, come to believe in him. That is faith and that is the way we know God.

When this happens to us, it is natural for us to address God as "Father" (Gal. 4:4-6). It is much more than assent; it is personal commitment. It is not believing *that* or *about* God; it is believing *in* God. Faith!

We come to know the will of God first by trusting him. Faith of this kind does not discourage other kinds of learning. The text before us places a high premium on the mind. Knowing the will of God is one of the evidences of faith. It cannot be known apart from the commitment of life. After we have made our commitment to him, we go on learning more about his will as we walk his way—proving what is the will of God.

Do you know people who maintain a very loose relationship with the church who want to dash in occasionally and get someone in the church to help them find out the will of God for a particular decision they have to make? It is not likely that this type of learning the will of God will help much. The will of God makes sense only to the person who is committed by faith to a life pleasing to God. People deceive themselves when they think they can use God when they need him and live as pagans the rest of the time. They would not understand the will of God if it were made known, and they would not be willing or able to do the will of God if they did understand it. It is known only in faith.

### Knowing by Regeneration

There are several terms in the Bible which teach that we undergo a transforming experience when we believe in God. God transforms us, changes us, in the process of forgiveness. Jesus told Nicodemus it was like being born again (John 3:3 f.), but Nicodemus did not grasp its meaning quickly. Paul did not speak of new birth, but rather used terms like "new creation" and "newness of life" (2 Cor. 5:17). Paul thought that the old Saul of Tarsus had died on the way to Damascus and Paul had been born out of the ruins to take his place. He had been buried with Christ and raised to "walk in newness of life" (Rom. 6:4).

The transformation of our lives in the work of God's grace opens up to us a new knowing of God's will. It frees our lives from the previous bondage to sin and fear. In reconciliation and faith, we see the will of God as we could not have seen it before. Paul saw this regenerate life as living "in Christ."

The Christian life is a different kind of life. The contrast between "life according to the flesh" and "life according to the spirit" (Rom. 8:5) clarifies it. Life according to the flesh is life before faith, oriented to one's own self; life according to the spirit is life by faith in Christ, oriented toward the Spirit. Obviously, all human life has a flesh element and a relationship with what we call spiritual. But the difference is in whether the guiding power of the life is orientation to one's own self without faith or to the Spirit of Jesus Christ by faith.

In the experience of regeneration, whether we think of the initial new birth or the process in life, we come to know the will of God.

## Knowing by Complete Dedication

You may never have thought that dedication is a way of coming to know. Paul stated, "Present your bodies as a living sacrifice, holy and acceptable to God . . . . that you may prove what is the will of God" (Rom. 12:1-2).

Our bodies are our whole selves, not merely our physical frames. The people had previously worshiped God by giving dead sacrifices; God wants us to dedicate ourselves as living sacrifices. We may find that living for God requires more courage and faith than dying a martyr's death. In this complete dedication to God, we learn what his will is.

If the will of God were merely an intellectual concept, we could learn it in the library or classroom. But it is more, it is a living religious conviction. We learn it only on the way.

Our ancestors who settled this land would have understood more easily than we do what our text is saying. They sold their holdings, gathered family and friends, braved the voyage by sea with its threatening storms, reefs, and a thousand other fears, to settle in a new land. In that new land, they lived and died and helped to establish a new nation which they hoped would bequeath more freedom to their children than the countries they had fled. They looked back and thanked God that they had the courage to make the effort. Even those who perished on the way were greater in their falling than many of those who survived merely by clinging to the security of the old homeland.

Christian believers make the commitment and enter the pilgrimage. They prove the will of God en route. Living by the will of God is not like taking a summer tour guided by a detailed travel plan outlined by a travel agent whose sources can route one around the hazards and road repairs to the best motels and restaurants. It is, rather, like a pilgrimage which begins in a dream or hope, then a setting out. There is a goal, but the road is not even marked in places. The pilgrims learn as they go.

When Paul wrote to the Roman Christians, he could not have known that his trip to Jerusalem was going to be a disaster. When the roof fell on him in Jerusalem, however, he did not abort his mission. He went on to Rome, but he went in chains. He learned that he could do the will of God in chains (Phil. 1:12-14). He had stated his plans, but others modified them.

Perhaps we want all of the details of the will of God before we start. That is a confession of unbelief. The railroad engineer leaves the East Coast to take a train to San Francisco (or at least, they used to do that). Along the way, his orders are revised and reissued. He does not change his destination; he goes on with whatever delays, detours, and schedule changes he encounters. Trains make deliveries, pick-ups; they encounter other trains on the tracks. Railroad engineers just don't drive trains across the country. They do all of these other things en route in order to get to their destination with the payload.

We begin the journey. We commit ourselves. We leave it to God to make his will known along the way.

## Knowing by Renouncing Conformity

The early Christians believed that a new age had dawned in Jesus Christ and that the old age was passing away. The new age was related to the kingdom of God. The term *age* is sometimes translated "world." The "world" can be the universe which God created, or it can be mankind fallen from God or in revolt against God. Obviously, we love the world which God loved; we want to transform the evil world (human culture) into God's new age.

The expression "do not be conformed to this world" means that we should not permit the world around us to shape our lives by its values, goals, prejudices, and the like. We had already been conformed to this world when we first learned there was a difference. So, we must first be delivered from that bondage. This is part of the meaning of deliverance, salvation from sin.

We have another problem as serious as individual bondage to sin. As members of society, we share in a corporate bondage. Our individual lives are always lived in communities of persons, some of which have centuries of tradition. These human collectives may be good or evil or a combination of the two. We are in them. We are conformed to them before we recognize them. They form the structure of human life. How can we renounce conformity to this age?

Acceptance of Christ means a new center of life, both individually and collectively. It requires a kind of renunciation in the beginning. In turning to God by faith, one does turn away from certain aspects of this world. We are not talking about asceticism or withdrawal from the world. Rather, we are speaking about being liberated from the slavery to these human structures so that we may exercise human freedom toward changing them.

The refusal to be conformed to this age requires a constant and vigilant struggle. One can easily fall into an equally dangerous nonconformity. This nonconformity is a very objectionable type of a new conformity and has been abundantly demonstrated in the years immediately past. One achieves no goal by merely being different. But breaking out of the blinding conformity to the present age can open the way for knowing more clearly what is God's will.

We get into the ruts without being aware of it. An executive illustrated this lesson of budgeting time to those he supervised in a training session. He casually mentioned twelve minutes for driving to work. They all lived in the same suburb and had to drive about the same distance to work. They immediately objected that the distance by freeway at the legal speed limit required twenty minutes and they had to drive it at the most crowded time of the day. He asked them if they had looked for alternate routes. They had not;

he had. He had found a little-traveled route which was much shorter. They had conformed, without critical reflection, to the popular idea that the freeway is the quickest way. We don't even consider "Christian options" in our daily living in many situations. We just follow along with the customs of our age.

Why don't you make a list of the major values of your life—how you spend your time and your money? Then, make a parallel list of Christian values, goals, and ways for investing time, talents, and resources. Compare them.

The present age subjects us to persuasive pressures to buy things we don't need and cannot afford. We yield to the pressure to live by the standards of other people without even considering whether the standards are appropriate for people with a commitment to God. We engage in our business or work according to the standards of others in the same work or business, without considering whether these standards are acceptable ethically.

We live in an age which is characterized by great diversity in terms of the national, racial, religious, economic, and social values and norms. We all know the prejudices and evils perpetuated by some of these cultural powers. We have the power to change these structures, at least to a degree, and thereby improve the lot of human life. Why conform to these powers when we could transform them?

These powers of our age blind and enslave us. Paul's admonition is that we seek to be free from this slavery and blindness so that we can live out of Christ's power. This is a way for knowing God's will.

## Knowing by Renewal of the Mind

The text stresses the transformation of our lives so that we may "prove what is the will of God." The primary means of this transformation is the "renewal of the mind."

The mind includes reason but is more than reason. It includes the whole faculty for knowing and understanding. We grasp some truth by reason, some by intuition, some by involvement, some by love, some by faith. The marvelous mind, *nous,* with which God has endowed us, is a means for knowing God's will.

The word for repentance, *metanoia,* means a change of mind. It is a change of mind toward God, sin, and self. It is a transforming change of one's life direction. Biblical faith allows no basis for the anti-intellectualism often so rampant in religious circles. The mind is God's good creation. One of the first signs of transformation from sin back into "the image of his Son" is this different attitude of mind. The bondage to sin blinds the mind; deliverance from sin frees the mind to serve God.

The liberation of the mind is like the removal of blindness. Minds in sin are "darkened" (Rom. 1:21). Christ's work of redemption in us frees us from this tyranny. Now we see!

In the Christian life, this liberation continues as one studies, reflects, talks with other believers, worships, and serves God. We have noted how Paul reflected in his letters how this learning and liberating process happens along the way. Christ renews our minds. He does not take them away from us. We do not surrender them. He frees our minds from bondage so we have them in full possession. We learn to think on Christ's values. "We have the mind of Christ" (1 Cor. 2:16).

We learn most of this in pilgrimage with others. We help each other remove the fear, lack of understanding, prejudice, and ignorance as we increasingly learn to love, understand, accept others, and grow in the knowledge of God and his purpose for our lives.

Jesus called his followers disciples, or learners. He was the Teacher. The Christian life is discipleship, learning the will of God while living the Christian life. The church is a school too. The mind is an endowment of great value. If we would know the will of God, we shall have to utilize our minds to the fullest. And often, it won't be in trying to grasp some new truth as much as it will be opening our minds so others can teach us what they have learned about living, forgiving, caring, and going on when there are more reasons for quitting.

Study is a legitimate Christian endeavor. The Scriptures afford a vast reservoir for learning the ways of God as other people have tried to walk in them. There is no substitute for biblical understanding and reflection on those truths. Much is to be learned from Christians of the past who learned God's will under different circumstances. History is a study with great rewards to Christians who would renew their minds in order to prove what the will of God is.

The renewal of the mind happens in the process of thinking about ethical decisions as they are confronted in life. Much of our previous discussion has been doctrinal. Paul devoted eleven chapters in Romans to such doctrinal discussions. The last five chapters of Romans deal with practical or ethical themes and personal matters. The text of Romans 12:1-2 is the transition. In other words, if his theological statements are true, then certain ethical implications are inevitable. In short, the renewal of the mind is related to the theological understanding of the faith (Rom. 1—11) and the making of ethical decisions (Rom. 12—15).

The renewing of the mind makes it possible to prove what the will of God is. What is the will of God? It is deciding what is right ethically and doing it.

## The Will of God as a Matter of Ethics

Anders Nygren said that Romans 12:1-2 is Paul's "basic rule of ethics."[1] There can be no doubt but that it stands not only as a transitional statement between the doctrinal and ethical themes of Romans but also it is a kind of principle introducing the ethical reflections.

This passage, however, is not a system of ethics; it is a series of illustrations about how a Christian decides what is right. It is not a set of rules but an important insight into those principles which play a part in ethics. This is important to our study because one aspect of the will of God is that we make right ethical decisions and then do what we decided. This is the will of God for us.

In recent years many ethicists have worked with a particular approach called situation ethics. Joseph Fletcher is one of the best known in this group, but there are many others of prominence. Situation ethics rejects the legalistic approach to ethical deciding and stresses two major themes: Love is the only guide in an ethical decision; and every decision is made within the situation guided only by love without rules. Joseph Fletcher is certainly correct in stressing the priority of love and the importance of the situation. But, in my judgment, he neglects the lessons learned in the past and passed on to us in the law, in culture, and in the teachings of Jesus. I think one can follow guiding principles, acknowledge the priority of love, and allow the specific situation its proper place in ethical thinking without being a legalist.

Our purpose here is not to present a comprehensive statement of Paul's ethics or ethical method. It is, rather, to show how he viewed the will of God as related to the Christian's view and practice of ethics.

In Romans 12—15, Paul stressed numerous themes of which the following appear to be basic: (1) ethical living involves a particular attitude toward and relationship with self, others, the church, and persons of different religious views; (2) love is the primary ethical motivation; (3) the Christian makes a distinction between good and evil; (4) the Christian follows Jesus' principle of nonretaliation; (5) the Ten Commandments are important and are fulfilled in love for the neighbor; (6) Christian ethics leads to a right relationship with the state; (7) ethics focuses on persons rather than principles as seen in the discussion about those weaker persons; (8) we make ethical decisions out of a basic belonging to the Lord.

Ethical thinking requires a right relationship with persons. We must have a modest but realistic estimate of ourselves. We must not be conceited or have low self-esteem. We should be honest in our self-appraisal (12:3). The other persons form the context for our appraisal and our own existence. Throughout the section, Paul spoke of our interdependence with others in the church which is like a body with many members (12:4-8). Christians decide ethical matters only in their relationships to others. Paul said much about loving the neighbor (13:8 ff.) and about persons with different religious views and practices (14:1 to 15:6). It is not clear whether these persons think of themselves as Christians. Doing the will of God in terms of making ethical decisions requires a considerate attitude toward all other persons.

Paul stressed the priority of love. Christian love is the intelligent, caring, self-giving attitude and behavior to other persons growing out of Christ's love for us. It is quite different from emotional attachment or sentimental "liking." It seeks to do that which is good for the other person. "Let love be genuine" (12:9); "love one another" (12:10); "he who loves his neighbor has fulfilled the law" (13:8). When we make ethical decisions, we do so out of genuine Christian love for persons. This is knowing and doing the will of God.

The Christian makes a discriminating distinction between good and evil: "Hate what is evil, hold fast to what is good" (12:9). Lists of virtues and vices tend to focus on immediate rather than permanent issues and tend to exaggerate minor themes at the expense of major ones. Some things are wrong: reveling, drunkenness, debauchery, licentiousness, quarreling, and jealousy (13:13). Other things are right: loving the neighbor and conducting ourselves "becomingly." We can distinguish between these opposites and seek the good in our own lives without imposing a legalistic ethic on others.

Nonretaliation is a basic Christian principle of ethics. Paul repeated the themes of Jesus: "Bless those who persecute you; bless and do not curse them . . . 'if your enemy is hungry, feed him; if he is thirsty, give him drink' " (12:14,20). The contrast between Jesus' teaching, here cited by Paul, and the law is significant. The law forbade murder; Jesus forbade hating or despising a person. The law forbade adultery; Jesus forbade lust. But Jesus went much further; he advocated no retaliation and an active love for that person against whom we would otherwise take vengeance. The person who retaliates invites retaliation. Retaliation invites escalation. The injury and estrangement increase. Jesus advocated, and Paul accepted, a corrective principle which would halt the escalation and reverse the process. There may be no other way in human relationships. Someone has to take the first step. Jesus and Paul indicated that the Christian is the one who knows what to do and has the ability to do it. Don't retaliate! This is God's will!

The Ten Commandments are still respectable guidelines and are summed up in the Christian phrase, "Love your neighbor"

(13:8-10). When we love our neighbors, we will not commit the acts prohibited in the law. To love the neighbor creates a positive environment for us both to do right. This is the will of God.

The Christian who thinks ethically has a positive attitude toward and participation in the state. This involves, at a minimum, obeying the laws and paying taxes (13:1-7). Paul had a positive attitude toward the Roman Empire. The author of Revelation, thirty-five years later, thought the same government was the embodiment of evil in his time. Paul would probably say today that Christians ought to pay their income taxes and obey the fifty-five mile per hour speed limit. Doesn't it seem strange to you that a person would be asking about the will of God for his life while breaking the laws of the state or cheating on taxes?

Christian ethics places a higher premium on persons than principles. Legalistic ethics would defend the rules and principles sometimes at the expense of persons. But my statement, "Christian ethics places a higher premium on persons than principles," is itself a principle and one worth preserving. Paul devoted a large part of this section to weaker persons who hold to different religious rules and practices (14:1 to 15:6). The guideline is that the stronger person can accept and handle the difference more easily than the weaker one, and the stronger must not lead the weaker person into stumbling. We noted Jesus' regard for the children. It is always the will of God that we consider other persons and refrain from attitudes or acts that would "put them down."

In the early fifties, a group of American tourists visited an Arab country. Missionary women met the group. They requested that the three women in the party not wear rouge and lipstick and wear head coverings while in their country. American customs in these areas were contrary to the customs of women in that culture. No morality was involved. The women obligingly did so. It was better for these woman to respect local customs than to insist upon their own. True, someone needs to teach these persons that no moral principles are involved in wearing cosmetics, but love called for the response since the other course may have been an occasion for offense.

Christian ethics grows out of a basic belonging to God. One could easily overlook the significant justification Paul gave for his ethical teachings, "We are the Lord's" (14:8). This belonging is a much needed corrective for the overly assertive selfishness of our time. The Christian does right because of a view of life—I belong to God and I want all others to. "You are not your own; you were bought with a price. So glorify God in your body" (1 Cor. 6:19-20). And again, Paul identified himself in terms of "the God to whom I belong and whom I worship" (Acts 27:23). How beautiful! Is it possible that persons in our time have been too concerned about the question, Who am I? and not quite concerned enough about Whose am I? We belong to God and to one another!

God's will is for us to do right. Doing right is possible only if we decide what is right. In any specific situation we can anticipate some uncertainty. To state glibly that we can always know what is right and do it would be misleading. But we can say with confidence that if we follow the discipline of belonging to God, belonging to others, praying, using our minds, and talking with others, we can discern, usually, what is right.

Doing right is a matter of ethics. It is the will of God.

# 7
# A Mystery—
# The Will of God Made Known

*For he has made known to us in all wisdom and insight* the mystery of his will, *according to his* purpose *which he set forth in Christ as* a plan for the fulness of time, *to unite all things in him, things in heaven and things on earth (Eph. 1:9-10).*

You have been aware of the difficulty we have in speaking clearly about some aspects of the will of God. God has revealed himself to us adequately enough for us to believe in him and obey him, but he remains concealed as well as revealed. God is mysterious. It is not strange, therefore, that we encounter this mystery when we talk of his will.

In biblical tradition, we believe that we know God only because he chose to reveal himself. He made that disclosure in the great events recorded in the Bible. He also inspired the prophets and apostles, his witnesses on the scene, to speak God's word on the basis of that revelation. The greatest revelatory event was Jesus Christ. He was the center of a cluster of events, which appear in biblical history like a great solar system. The author of Ephesians had the advantage over earlier witnesses. He lived after the event of Jesus Christ had become reasonably clear. He wrote that God "has made known to us . . . the mystery of his will" (1:9).

We can speak much more clearly now about the will of God, and we can learn a great deal about that mystery from the other biblical events which preceded it. We shall look at one of those events in the Old Testament, the saga of Joseph. Then we shall consider Peter's interpretation of the death and resurrection of Jesus Christ as understood shortly after the resurrection.

## The Mystery of the Will of God to a Slave in Egypt

"As for you, you meant evil against me; but God meant it for good, to bring it about that many people should be kept alive, as they are today. So do not fear; I will provide for you and your little ones" (Gen. 50:20-21).

The Joseph saga is an intriguing and suspense-filled adventure story. It is a historical narrative of great significance that gives a detailed and accurate look into the intricacies of patriarchal life and affords us the opportunity of looking in on both Canaan and Egypt. But that is not the reason for its inclusion in Genesis.

The author of Genesis was a straightforward person. I would not want him as my biographer. He told about the frailties, crimes, the weak and despicable, just as readily as he told about the heroic and the good. But that is not the reason he told us about Joseph.

The narrative about Joseph and his older brothers was included in Genesis because of the profound theological insight into the mystery of the providence of God which was at work even within the setting of criminal activity.

Joseph was a dreamer. He was also ambitious. He was a bit offensive to his older brothers. Even his father was uneasy when Joseph dreamed that someday the whole family would bow down to him. His brothers despised him. Joseph was a bit naive; he taunted his brothers.

The older brothers wanted to kill him. When he came out to them near Dothan, they decided that the time had come for them to get rid of him. Reuben connived to save Joseph's life and persuaded them to throw him into a pit. It was Judah who suggested the cold alternative to murder—sell him into slavery. His rationale was that killing him would turn no profit; selling him into slavery would. And, too, there was an instinctive fear, or superstition, about killing "our brother." That word, brother, seems out of place in such a grim context.

Joseph's rise to power in Egypt was not a smooth success story. He arrived in Egypt with scarcely anything left but his chastity, and Potiphar's wife wanted that. Joseph was "handsome and good-looking," but he was also a man of principle. He refused her—a feat in itself. After all, he was a slave a long way from home, who would ever know? His reason for refusing her was his obligation to Potiphar and the trust placed in him. The violation of that trust would have been a "sin against God" (Gen. 39:9).

When slave boys received the masters' wives' invitations to "lie with me," (39:7), it was either the bed or the prison, if not the gallows. But, Joseph was nimble; like a cat when thrown, he landed on his feet. His dreams had gotten him into trouble in the first place; now his interpretation of dreams would be the means not only of survival but also of triumph. Joseph saw the meaning of the pharaoh's dreams—seven years of bountiful harvests followed by seven years of famine. So Joseph became the official in charge of agricultural production, storage, and distribution.

Power of this type does not fall to the "jolly good fellows." It falls into the hands of the ambitious, the strong, the crafty, and the ruthless; or rather, they seize it. Ancient Egypt had anticipated our modern era in this regard and Joseph qualified.

The famine arrived on schedule. It was severe, but Joseph had prepared Egypt. When the famine descended on the hill country of Palestine, Joseph's brothers went to Egypt for food.

The older brothers did not recognize Joseph. He was only a lad when they had sold him. Joseph recognized them, however; they were already grown and bearded when he had left. Joseph deceived them, tricked them, and framed them by having a silver cup "planted" in their luggage. The resultant charge of theft could have gotten one of them the death penalty. Now, I don't want to deny to Joseph any family affection, which is obvious later, but I do wish to show that Joseph was no sentimental soul who could forget the past crime with a shrug of the shoulders.

The story of Joseph is not a sentimental account of a family reunion in which Joseph, now grown, said something like, "Forget it, boys will be boys." He had been the victim of a cruel crime. His treacherous older brothers had sold him into slavery; Joseph had gagged on the bitter fruit of their act for many years. Not only had he been denied the association with his family, so important in the patriarchal society, but he had also been in danger for his life. (Perhaps you should reread Genesis 37—50 to be sure I am being faithful to the text. Note that one-fourth of the entire book deals with Joseph.)

Power had changed Joseph. No naive boy—that Joseph. He could have had their heads severed from their shoulders and been applauded for it. He probably thought about it. But he didn't do it. We miss the meaning of these narratives when we overdo the family reunion. Look at Joseph's reasoning.

Joseph bowed to a power greater than he and his brothers. Twice in the narrative, Joseph stated this profound insight—this mystery. When he first saw it, he said, "so it was not you who sent me here, *but God*" (45:8). Then again at the end of the saga, the end of Genesis, he repeated it, "As for you, you meant evil against me; *but God* meant it for good" (50:20). Notice the depth of mystery grasped momentarily in those two words, "But God"! Years of hardship, resentment if not bitterness, struggle, questions about a human crime! An incredible rise to power! A new situation not entirely of his own making! A coming together of estranged "brothers!" Joseph saw it.

We don't know when Joseph saw it or how God led him to see it. But years of reflection had prepared him for it. He had not forgotten the crime. He restated their evil intent; he never did forget that it was a crime. It was forever a crime! But God had a purpose for Israel which he would not give up merely because of a crime. Joseph saw briefly, albeit incompletely, the mysterious providence of God. He could only say, "you meant evil . . . but God meant it for good."

Have you ever been present when a community was devastated by a fire, storm, flood, hurricane, or earthquake? Did you notice how community prejudices were temporarily forgotten? Did you notice that the distinction between the rich and the poor vanished for a while? Did you notice how the banker and the pauper worked side by side to salvage what was left? Isn't it strange how calamity can destroy the artificial barriers we have constructed? Then we see ourselves as we really are. Death does it in families. Estrangement, for whatever reason, disappears at least momentarily when the death of a loved one brings the persons to see that the bonds which bind them are stronger than their differences.

The presence of God, however he may appear, does the same thing; he shocks us into the awareness that he and his will make all other factors secondary. Joseph saw the hand of God in his and his brothers' lives. God's will for them was greater than any differences which had separated them. Joseph laid aside or overcame his hostile feelings toward them. He forgave them! He did it because of the insight into this mystery of God's will. When God is working to redeem us, it becomes obvious that God's grace is adequate enough to include both the victims and the perpetrators of crimes.

God guides us to his gracious goal even through the bewildering maze of human history with all of its guilt. Somehow his saving work is loving enough to include sinful men and women along with their sinful acts. God maintains a radical secrecy and silence about his ways. Only on rare occasions, like this one of Joseph and his brothers, does he pull back the curtain for a moment so that we can glimpse his providential work.

We must resist the temptation of going back to Dothan and pulling God in as an accomplice to the brothers' crime. God was no slave-trader. The older brothers were. Joseph never blurred the distinction between God and his brothers.

Joseph did not offer the interpretation that their crime was really a "blessing in disguise." This error is of more recent vintage. Joseph held in stark contrast the unexplainable facts: human crime and a providential working of God.

The "blessing in disguise" interpretation of our misfortunes is a well-meaning habit of careless thinkers. On one occasion, a church community was torn by internal strife. Strong-willed persons differed. They said harsh things about each other and finally in anger divided their congregation. Since theirs was a growing community, both factions survived in two congregations that did increase in numbers. Later, people denied their guilt for the initial division by seeing it as the leadership of God. Two churches instead of one! They said, "God works in a mysterious way!" I wonder how much

God has to do with this type of church growth. Church splits are not "blessings in disguise"; they are tragic upheavals with damaging consequences which last for generations. There are better ways for starting new congregations.

It is very dangerous for us to drag God in to take the blame for our wrongs. Joseph refused to do it. On an occasion years ago, I stood with a family in the time of deep grief. The aging mother had died in a horrible home accident—a fire. On three occasions I had heard one member of the family point out the danger and urge the installation of a simple safety device which would have prevented the accident. The other members refused. On the day when we all stood speechless in grief, one member of that family said, "Why did God take her this way?" In that setting, it seemed inappropriate to say anything. We all need comfort in times of sorrow, but do we want to blame God for our mistakes?

Perhaps we shall never understand the mystery, but some light appeared in the history of Israel. The suffering of Israel, which seemed so difficult, appeared to be redemptive suffering. Why it should be we don't seem to know. But the suffering servant of Isaiah (see chapter 53) reveals an insight into the mystery which will later be more fully disclosed in Christ's suffering. Apparently, God somehow works for redemption within those who do suffer on behalf of others.

We cannot fathom the love of God, so we have trouble with the will of God. How could God work to redeem the older brothers through the suffering of Joseph, the victim of their crime?

One of God's means of redemption was Joseph's willingness to forgive his brothers. Sometimes God achieves his will in the lives of persons through the forgiveness of other persons. We are not talking about what God could have done; we are speaking, rather, about what he actually did. Presumably, God could have done it some other way; actually, he worked his will for Israel by means of Joseph's forgiveness. Joseph suffered on behalf of his family, but he didn't understand it until the brothers appeared before him. If we would grasp the meaning of God's will, we must move beyond the mere demand for justice into the realm of mercy, love, and grace.

Members of three families sat in the emergency waiting room of the hospital. They anxiously waited for word about family members who had been severely injured in a three-car accident. One man was dead; a person from each of the other families was dying. The news media reported the police to have said that the two younger drivers had been drag racing on a city street. One of them seemingly lost control for a moment; there was a head-on accident. The man killed instantly was the father of four; his wife and three children were injured. The aging mother of the deceased man sat in the waiting room. The father of the young driver of the vehicle which had killed her son was in the same room. He went to the aging woman, knelt, and said something to her. She reached her hand over and placed it on his shoulder and said, "Oh no, we would never feel that way. We are concerned for you and your son too."

The two others died within the week. One was the young driver of the other car. We would not want to interpret this event so as to deny the human responsibility (although one person did say to me, "God knew what he was doing"), but we see in the forgiving spirit of one of the victims the beginning of the healing process. Forgiveness is according to the will of God. He often accomplishes his will through our forgiving. Forgiving involves suffering. The question is not about God's will in the event; the question has to do with what God wills me to do in the situation as it is.

And so, mystery remains. We have learned a lesson about the mystery of God's will. God is active in human history. He does look ahead and work for our salvation. Even in our reverses and when we are victims of crime, God does not abandon us but is at work on our behalf. But he may also be working to save those who victimize us. He loves them too. God does not excuse their crimes or pretend that the crimes don't matter. *But God!*

Joseph knew the persons whose crime led to his suffering. This is not always the case with others. Human crime becomes a part of collective living. It takes the form of prejudice, nationalism, racial and religious hate, economic oppression, and a host of others. These crimes become entrenched in social structures. Social collectives are even more cruel than identifiable brothers who sell slaves. They are difficult to identify, more difficult to change. As we work to deliver people from any slavery, the story of Joseph tells us that God also works toward the same end.

We see the hand of God more clearly in retrospect. Our personal interpretations of the past may be wrong, but as human beings we make them. Let us be guided by the biblical narratives to interpret our own situations wisely. God will make known to us the mystery of his will.

## The Will of God in Cross and Resurrection

"Jesus of Nazareth, a man attested to you by God with mighty works and wonders and signs which God did through him in your midst, as you yourselves know—this Jesus, delivered up according to the definite plan and foreknowledge of God, you crucified and killed by the hands of lawless men. But God raised him up. Repent, and be baptized everyone of you in the name of Jesus Christ for the forgiveness of your sins; and you shall receive the gift of the Holy Spirit" (Acts 2:22-24,38).

Peter stressed the following themes in his preaching at Pentecost: (1) Jesus of Nazareth had shown the presence of God in his life by working wonders; (2) his death had been "according to the definite plan and foreknowledge of God"; (3) Jesus had been crucified and "killed by the hands of lawless men"; (4) but God had raised Jesus from the dead; (5) God had exalted Jesus to the role of Lord and Christ; and (6) salvation has been given through Christ to those who repent. This summary is quite like Paul's summary in which he stressed "that Christ died for our sins in accordance with the scriptures . . . he was raised on the third day" (1 Cor. 15:3-4).

Peter spoke of the mystery. He was sure of two facts: Lawless men had killed Jesus, and Jesus' death was according to "the definite plan and foreknowledge of God.'' How could the will of God and a crime of men coincide in this event?

Jesus appeared to have failed at the cross. His disciples thought so. They had been thrilled with Jesus' teaching and wonders. They had seen him heal the sick and restore sight to the blind. But he was dead. Their excitement of anticipation about his kingdom died on the cross.

''But God raised him up'' (Acts 2:24). Again, we see that radical turning in the words ''but God.'' The resurrection transformed apparent defeat into victory. The first Easter is the turning point of history. God changed the whole universe when he raised Jesus from the dead. Resurrection means more than ''Jesus is alive.'' Lazarus was alive, but he died again. Jesus is alive forevermore. But, even more, the resurrection meant that Jesus really is the Son of God. God was really present in Jesus' life. The cross stands as the ultimate contradiction, the love of God and the rejection by sinful people, hope and despair, victory and defeat. The resurrection stands as the ultimate affirmation, ''but God''!

Peter preached this sermon seven weeks after the resurrection. There had hardly been time for the disciples to theologize about these events. Peter's declaration included the mystery without attempt at explanation.

Since Peter's time, the theologians of the church have worked hard to explain, or even illustrate, the saving work of God in Christ. But mystery still remains. The saving event is like a diamond which reflects its beauty from many angles but does not reveal all of its beauty to any one observer or from any single viewpoint. It is a sacrificial act from Christ's standpoint, but it would hardly be correct to say that God sacrificed Jesus. Christ died for our sins, but the idea of substitution is not adequate for stating the mystery. The event stands as a judgment on sin, but it is not a simple case of God punishing Jesus for someone else's sins. Christians universally proclaim the salvation act even though our explanations fall short.

The incarnation gives us a clue. The death of Christ is the saving event because of who he was, Son of God and genuine man. As a person who had encountered hostility for his faithfulness to the Father, Jesus went to the cross at the hands of those whom he came to save. There were no innocent bystanders at the cross. Everyone was involved in one way or another, just as we are today. And, there was one other involved, whose unseen hand moves in history. *But God.*

The text insists on human responsibility in an event in which God worked for our salvation. Christ died not only on our behalf but also by our hands. His atoning work becomes effective for us individually precisely when we recognize our responsibility. Repentance, which is turning to God from sin, is a change of mind about God, ourselves, and our sin. The confession of sin is part of its cure. The denial of responsibility is evidence of continuing estrangement from God. Adam blamed Eve and finally God, "the woman whom thou gavest to be with me" (Gen. 3:12). Eve blamed the serpent. There are those who deny their sin by blaming biological transmission of sin from Adam and our parents. The cross prompts us to pray, "God be merciful to me, a sinner."

The text also insists on God's role in the saving work of Christ. If God were not in Christ's work, the cross would have been merely another instance of a grave injustice in which a mob lynched an innocent person.

The mystery is that God worked for our salvation in events of human history. We must allow room in our understanding of these events for both man's responsible acts and God's redeeming work. This is very important in talking about the will of God. For instance, in our individual lives we may have done something careless or wrong in which suffering resulted. It was our fault, no one else's. But God may have worked with us or others in those experiences in a way that was redemptive.

A person once received a very painful, though minor, injury in a home accident. He injured himself in a moment of thoughtlessness. When he was in the hospital, he shared his room with a person who had not made a commitment of his life to Christ. This injured man,

through sharing his faith, witnessed a rather remarkable transformation in the life of the other person. Later, when telling this
experience, he commented, "Now I can see why God hurt me in the
accident. It hurt so much at the time, I couldn't understand. Now I
do." Is that a fair statement? Is it a responsible statement?

In our culture of the late twentieth century, young people at
about age sixteen must learn to drive an automobile. It is a practical
necessity and has become a symbol of dawning maturity. I provided a safe car, driver's education, adequate insurance, and anxious fatherly instruction. I said to my son, "An automobile can be a
dangerous weapon. I give you the freedom to drive, but you are
responsible for the vehicle, the persons with you, and any other
persons or property you may encounter along the way. The police
officer thinks you are a safe driver. He passed you on your driver's
test. So, I give you permission to drive the car. You are responsible."

Now, let's suppose that in a moment of carelessness my son took
a dare and drove fast. Suppose he had an accident which caused
fatalities. Would it be fair to say, "Morris Ashcraft permitted his
son to cause the fatal accident?" Would it not be fairer to say,
"Mark betrayed his father's trust"? We are not speaking about
legal responsibility, who gets sued. We are talking about moral
responsibility. In like manner it does not seem right to say that God
causes or permits the evil acts of men. In creation, God gave us
freedom. He did not give us permission to do wrong. In fact, we
betray the Father's trust when we do wrong. But God may still have
a way of working his redemptive purpose through or within the
events and the persons involved.

### The Mystery of God's Will Made Known

And to make all men see what is the *plan of the mystery hidden for
ages* in God who created all things; that through the church the
manifold wisdom of God might now be made known to the principalities and powers in the heavenly places. This was according to

the *eternal purpose* which he has realized in Christ Jesus our Lord (Eph. 3:9-11, author's italics).

We have noted the mystery of God's will made known in the history of Israel and then declared in the preaching of the apostle Peter. The author of Ephesians wrote about thirty or thirty-five years after Peter's sermon. He speaks of the mystery of God's will in a much more detailed way. He can do so because he has been able to see what God was doing in the life of the early church. The revealed mystery touches a number of very important themes.

I will not burden you at this time with minute distinctions among the terms used. The great themes in broad outline are heavy enough to consume all of our energy for the moment. Note, however, the following phrases: "he destined us in love" (Eph. 1:5); "according to the *purpose of his will*" (1:5); "redemption" (1:7); "the mystery of his will" and "according to his *purpose* which he set forth in Christ" (1:9); a *"plan for the fulness of time"* (1:10); the *"purpose of him who* accomplishes all things *according to the counsel of his will"* (1:11). Note the "mystery of Christ" (3:4), *"the plan of the mystery hidden for ages* in God" (3:9), is to be "made known . . . *through the church"* (3:10). This was *according to the eternal purpose* which he has realized in Christ Jesus our Lord" (3:11) [Italics mine].

The mystery about the will of God now made known in Christ clarifies many questions and uncertainties, such as the doctrine of election; the inclusion of the Gentiles as the elect; the nature of salvation achieved through Christ's death. The mystery of God's will as an eternal purpose including all of God's creation and the role of the church in the eternal purpose of God are also clarified.

The biblical idea of election has been clarified in the disclosure of the mystery of God's will. Israel was the elect people. Election, an expression of God's will, had been for service, not privilege. The doctrine has been greatly misunderstood, leading to considerable damage. The author of Ephesians taught that all along election had been the expression of God's love, choosing people to be holy and blameless. Through his people he intended to bless all the families of the earth.

Now the revealed mystery is that the *Gentiles are included* in election. "We who first hoped" (1:12) are Hebrews. "You also" are the Gentiles (1:13). The rest of chapter one and all of chapter two deal with this theme. The Gentiles "heard the word of truth" as the Hebrews had; it was to them the "gospel of your salvation"; the Gentiles "believed in him"; they were "sealed with the promised Holy Spirit"; and they had received the "guarantee of" the future inheritance (1:13-14), the fullness of salvation. Gentiles have received salvation according to the will of God. The "mystery of Christ" (3:4) made known is that the Gentiles are "fellow heirs, members of the same body, and partakers of the promise in Christ Jesus through the gospel" (3:6). This had been God's will through the ages and was fully made known in Christ.

Salvation is a relationship with God known as "redemption" and "forgiveness" achieved through the blood of Christ (1:7). God's will is that all people everywhere shall be reconciled to him and to one another. Christ's suffering was the focus of the redeeming act.

The eternal purpose *"set forth in Christ"* (1:9) is *our salvation.* The "plan" (3:9) is for the church to make this eternal purpose known to all the world. God's will includes all creation, "to unite all things in him, things in heaven and things on earth" (1:10). The purpose of God is grander than any idea the church has held about it.

The will of God is that the *church* shall be the agency by which and in which his purpose is to be achieved. The church (3:10) can make God's will known. We think first of the proclamation of the gospel to the world, and this is basic. But we need to note that salvation takes place within those who are together in the church. A large part of the church's proclamation is the demonstration of the redeemed lives of individuals and the redeemed community. The text calls for an expanded vision of the church.

The "eternal purpose" of God which has been revealed is now

being "realized in Christ Jesus our Lord" (3:11). It is a *present reality*. The author of Ephesians could see it happening. The community of the redeemed and the redeeming! This is the church.

## Redemptive Suffering

The great letter to the Ephesians begins with the notice that our salvation, the great plan of God, has been achieved through the death of Christ (1:7). The author was in prison when he wrote the letter. The church will achieve its mission through the crucible of redemptive suffering.

We noted how Joseph was the agent through whose suffering God saved Israel from the famine and, hence, for their destiny. Joseph suffered at their hands and forgave because he saw God's purpose. We noted that Peter pointed out the saving work of God through Christ's suffering and went on to witness for Christ when it was dangerous to do so.

Isaiah saw the theme of redemptive suffering. Some believe that he predicted the coming of Jesus Christ. Every Christian who reads Isaiah 53 sees it as a description of Jesus' suffering whether Isaiah intended it to be that specific. Others see the suffering Israel in the drama. Israel's suffering had been prolonged, agonizing, and difficult to understand. The prophet then glimpsed the theme of salvation—Israel's suffering brought salvation to others. The writers of the Old Testament, therefore, interpreted the suffering itself as being willed by God. And perhaps this is so. But God often worked his redemptive purpose through human suffering which appeared to be of human origin. This leaves us with the mystery of how God in his providence works in conjunction with our human freedom.

If you have ever walked down a railroad track, you have seen an illustration that may help. While walking on the cross ties between the two rails you looked behind you and the two rails appeared to merge into one. Then you look into the distance ahead of you and the same illusion occurs. Perhaps this happens to us when we look into the distant past or future. We can see clearly the human side and think we can see evidence of God's hand in history when we look at events close by. But when we look into the past, we lose sight of the human part and see primarily God's role. I think this tends to happen also when we look into the distant future.

God works for the achievement of his purpose in ways that are hidden to us and sometimes in ways that include our actions, even our mistakes. We cannot always explain.

The mystery remains? No. He has shown us the mystery in Christ. God's purpose for our salvation and that of all other persons throughout the world is revealed in Christ. And the church is to be involved in the task. And God works at it too.

# 8
# The Plan—
# The Will of God as a Plan for the Ages

*To me, though I am the very least of all the saints, this grace was
given, to preach to the Gentiles the unsearchable riches of Christ,
and to make all men see what is the plan of the mystery hidden for
ages in God who created all things; that through the church the
manifold wisdom of God might now be made known . . . . This
was according to the eternal purpose which he has realized in Christ
Jesus our Lord"* (Eph. 3:8-11, author's italics).

The Mediterranean Sea is about two thousand miles long and
hundreds of miles wide. It was a vast body of water to the early
Phoenician mariners who sailed across it. But in comparison to the
vastness of the Atlantic and Pacific Oceans it is an inland lake. Can
you imagine the thrill and awe when those sailors ventured through
the Straits of Gibraltar and first learned of the awesome vastness of
the Atlantic Ocean?

We have been dealing with the will of God primarily in terms of
God's will for our individual lives and for our collective living in
families and communities like the churches in which we learned of
God and try to worship him. The author of Ephesians, like the
Phoenician sailors who ventured through the straits and out into
the larger ocean, ventured out of an individualistic view of God's
will into a comprehensive purpose of God for all creation and all
ages. He also saw more than a purpose; he saw a plan already in
action for achieving that purpose. The plan had been hidden in
mystery, but Jesus Christ made it known.

The Christian era began in a series of dramatic events. Jesus of
Nazareth, like a tremendous earthquake, shook the world. Around

100

him was a cluster of related events which attended the initiation of the Christian faith. The little land of Palestine was the epicenter; the quakes continue to shake the world.

Seemingly the vast ocean of time and eternity, like the sand in an hourglass, came to a narrow focus in Jesus' life and then spread out into all eternity. We might think of Jesus Christ as a new star which suddenly appeared and drew all others into orbit around itself. He gave all creation not only its orbit and direction but also its reason for being.

We have already spoken of the North Star, a star that appears to remain fixed while others revolve in their orbits around it. The North Star is one constant navigational fix that never varies! But Jesus Christ is more than a guide in the universe; he is the center of gravity which holds all parts of reality together (Col. 1:17).

Jesus Christ is not a discovery; he is the revelation of God. God took the initiative and disclosed himself to us, his creatures. The author of Ephesians was one of those witnesses privileged to see this marvelous revelation in history.

When we started our journey, I suggested that we begin with Christ. Then Paul told us about personal commitment to God's will. We are far enough away from the smoke of the city that we can now see stars in the clear atmosphere that we never knew existed. We were rightly concerned with our individual lives under the will of God; we never dreamed that the entire universe was also involved.

The author of Ephesians also thought first in terms of his own personal salvation. Then, later in the life and mission of the church, it became clear to him that God's work of redemption was a grand plan that included all of history and all of the world. Obviously, it had been God's plan all of the time, but it had remained hidden. Then, God made known this mystery of the ages. It was his eternal plan, his purpose, the will of God. The author sees himself as one solitary, frail, emprisoned old man but related to that cosmic plan.

Other biblical writers had glimpsed something of this plan.

Isaiah and Jeremiah had been able to see beyond the borders of tiny Israel, and they saw something of the purpose of God to include the other nations. Paul had himself, in a poetic moment, suggested that the saving work of Christ in some way embraced all creation (Rom. 8:18-25). The universal authority of Christ appears in several places (Phil. 2:10,11; Col. 1:20). But it is here in Ephesians that the statement of God's plan is clearest.

The author of Ephesians saw all reality through the telescope of God's saving plan. The whole world! Now we have to remember our lessons in interpretation. One use of the word *world* applies to fallen human culture. This was in his mind when John warned us against "this world." It was this sinful world in its revolt against God. But, we do not hate the world which God so loved and for which Christ died. We must not disparage God's world.

The gospel of salvation embraces the whole world and all of time and eternity. We often grossly understate our case when we speak of it. We often carelessly handle the gospel as if it were a mild devotional talk given to a small group of tired religious folk. The gospel is the good news from God that he wills to save all creation through Jesus Christ. The gospel is the very power to bring it about.

God's plan is infinitely more complex and grand than any human achievement. Look at the vast network of electronic equipment and specially trained personnel which are at work around the clock every day in the year to direct the aircraft through the skies. It is an amazing system. An operator in Kansas City directs a crew of an aircraft to remain an additional thirty minutes on the ramp. He is preventing a "stack-up" in the sky around Chicago because someone else told him when other aircraft left Pittsburgh, Minneapolis, and Atlanta. One lone operator has an importance beyond our calculation. The whole system depends on such persons. Paul had suddenly become aware of such a larger network of God—the grand plan for the ages—and his small station within it.

## A Personal Plan

Jesus Christ portrayed the heavenly Father as a shepherd looking for his lost sheep. His searching was motivated by his love, not the value of the sheep. God's personal love for each of his creatures is unique to Christianity. We speak of God's love (Eph. 1:5), his "grace" (1:7), and the "purpose of his will" (1:5). These are all very personal terms. Any discussion of God's will must be in personal terms. Even when speaking of the cosmic plan, it would not be God's plan if it became a law or principle or impersonal plan.

God's plan is personal because it involves human beings. It is not a scientific principle discernible by investigation or experiment. It is not a moral law discoverable by moral speculation. It is revealed only to persons who are addressed by the will of God. It is known only in personal response. It is not legalism. It is a personal conviction.

## A Revealed Plan

The author of Ephesians did not claim to have discovered God's plan; rather, the knowledge came with saving revelation. Christian faith is a response to God as revealed in Jesus Christ. We make no claim to superior religious insight. We do not claim that our missionary plans are the best. We acknowledge the moral concepts in other religions. Christian faith is based on the belief that God has revealed himself uniquely and most fully in Christ.

When the church loses sight of the revealed plan of God for the ages and its own part in that plan, it tends to substitute its own plan for God's plan. Then, of course, it seeks to perpetuate its own organization like any other human collective, such as labor unions or political parties. Then, missionary work is ecclesiastical colonialism; churches engage in mission activity when it is to their advantage to do so. Not so, the church that follows Christ. A church going its own way does not deserve to be called a "church."

## A Redemptive Plan

We have sinned against God our Creator. We have corrupted creation in the process. We have introduced a foreign element, like a virus, into the bloodstream of creation. This disease has become epidemic. Human life, intended for harmonious relationship with God and with the rest of the human family, has become distorted, perverted, estranged, destructive, and lost.

God's redemptive work starts with each individual and reaches out to others and finally to all creation. He wills to reconcile all "things in heaven and things on earth" (Eph. 1:10; 3:10) to himself. So revelation and reconciliation are inseparable if not actually the same. God always reveals himself in order to redeem—never for any other reason.

## A Christ-Centered Plan

This eternal purpose of God has been "realized in Christ Jesus our Lord" (3:11). God "was in Christ" (2 Cor. 5:19, KJV). In him the "fulness of God" was pleased to dwell (Col. 1:19). Christ determines our view of God and history. In Christ, God has "set forth" his "plan for the fulness of time" (Eph. 1:10).

When we seek to know God's will for our individual lives and for the church or to understand God's will in the world, we shall always be on the right track if we first find our way in Christ.

## A Historic Plan

Christian faith is grounded in historical events. This is not so with many other great religious systems. Buddhism and Hinduism, for instance, are reflective and meditative in nature; history is not important. They even seek to escape history. Biblical faith always looks to the continuum of history for God's revelation. God showed himself in the great events, such as the Exodus and the incarnation. The grand plan of God's will is a plan involving history, all of history.

Jesus Christ is the center of that history. The expression "fulness of time" (Eph. 1:10; Gal. 4:4, KJV) reflects the belief that God had spoken in history before Christ in a way leading up to his full revelation: "The Word became flesh" (John 1:14). Biblical faith holds men and women responsible for their roles in history, but it also allows for the working of God within history. In biblical faith, history moves from the creation to a consummation with the Christ at the center; there is no cyclical view of time in the Bible.

The old covenant is important, therefore, but not final. Jesus Christ in history points the way to eternity. The old covenant had prepared the world for the coming of Christ. Now, that he has come, it becomes obvious that God's plan is far grander than people had previously thought. All the world is included.

God who created the world is concerned about all of history and all people. We have looked at Christendom, as if God cared only for those of the Christian religion. That is as erroneous as the previously held notion that he cared only for the Hebrews. Jesus Christ is historical; he is also historic.[1] All of history is in the scope of his mission.

## An Eternal Plan

The expression "before the foundation of the world" (Eph. 1:4), though difficult, is clarified by the declaration that God's "eternal purpose" includes the Gentiles and is realized "in Christ Jesus" (3:11). The doctrine of election implied in "before the foundation of the world" has not been easy for us. But the biblical writer intended to show that God was not caught unawares; our salvation was not an afterthought. God's intention to lead us to our destiny is as abiding as his love for us, without limit in beginning or end.

## A Universal Plan

God's redeeming work extends beyond human life to all of creation (1:10)—the universe. This does not necessarily mean that everything will be saved; it may mean that everything is potentially savable. We may be included, but we may choose to exclude ourselves.

If God chose Israel to be his agent in reaching the rest of the world, it is reasonable to see the Christian understanding that all creation is potentially savable. The church witnessed the expansion from Jew to Gentile. The New Testament writers spoke of the dawning of a new age; Jesus had pointed in that direction. The next step points into the future and to the fact that God's plan includes all people.

## A Cosmic Plan

We have already noted how God's plan of redemption moves beyond human beings in their individual and collective responses to a kind of redemption of creation (1:10). Note also that this plan includes "principalities and powers in the heavenly places" (3:10). The world view prevalent in Asia Minor at the time Ephesians was written paid much attention to that realm above the earth in which it was believed such powers dwelt. The author, in using this terminology, meant to include all reality—earthy and heavenly—in God's redeeming work.

Jesus taught us to pray that his will may be done on earth as it was being done in heaven. That seems to mean heaven where only God and his faithful beings are. This idea in Ephesians may include even hostile powers. Speculation on this would lead into strange regions, but it is important to think of the cosmic nature of God's redeeming work which we know as individuals and families in our brief lifespans.

## A Church-Involved Plan

This plan of God for the ages included the church as God's agency for making the mystery known. The church is, of course, that "body of Christ," or the church universal so prevalent in Ephesians and Colossians. It is the family or "household of God" (Eph. 2:19). It is *"one"* (4:4).

The church universal is not some ideal or spiritual reality; it is the living historical body of Christ which originated in the life, death, and resurrection of Jesus Christ. It lives through the generations. The church universal is present in every local congregation that deserves to be called "a church." It comes into existence when God calls men and women and children through the gospel to believe in him. They come together into a family relationship, a church.

The church universal is a living reality, revealed or obscured in local churches, but real. Numerous organizations, denominations, missionary societies, and so forth carry on work that originated in the church universal. They may not be under the direct control of a church. They may represent the church. But, it behooves us all, organizations and churches alike, to investigate how closely we are related to the church universal, this body of Christ to which God entrusted his plan for the ages.

In our day, we think of holding membership in a church and contributing some time and a little money so the church can carry on its task. Many of us seem to think that the church can employ ministers and pay them to do this purpose which God has for the church. The missionaries are assigned the task of exporting our religion. This latent attitude may well be a denial of the church rather than service to it.

One cannot tell the "good news" unless it is "good" to the one telling it. The bearer of good news wears a smile on the face and reveals an enthusiasm without words. It is an impotent act when a religious advocate tells a world about religious faith without a winsome personal enthusiasm born of commitment and involvement.

It may be that our local churches are more like religious clubs in which we gather with people "like us" to enjoy one another and go back home or to work with less burden. If this is so, then we may have to undergo a revolution in our lives and thinking before we can grasp the purpose of God or participate in it.

The church is the family of God, the body of Christ, the community of the Holy Spirit. It lives out of God's power and purpose. It reaches out to give God's love and salvation to all persons. It is not an organization to export its own brand of religious merchandise. The church is not an imperial body colonizing the pagan world for its own growth or profit. It is Jesus' body giving itself away, perhaps through redemptive suffering.

When we speak of the church fulfilling the purpose of God, in our mind-set we think of church growth and missionary efforts. These are important, but they grow out of something that happens first in the church. The church not only bears the good news but also it lives on the good news. Redemption takes place in the lives of those who are drawn together in the churches. These communities of people fulfill the will of God by their own demonstration of love within their fellowships and to the others still outside. Only when this transformation is taking place can churches proclaim beyond themselves in achieving this marvelous purpose or will of God for the ages.

## A Single Plan

God's will is a unity since God is one. The great unity passage (Eph. 4:4-6) stresses the oneness of God, the Spirit, the body, hope, faith, baptism.

There is one gospel of salvation. In the New Testament, there are no other gospels (Gal. 1:6-9). The one gospel is the "unsearchable riches of Christ" (Eph. 3:8). The good news brings power to save (Rom. 1:16); nothing else does. The exclusivism in Christian faith is derived from the oneness of God. This exclusivism is all-inclusive. No one is excluded; the gospel speaks to all persons everywhere: love is all-inclusive.

There is no other plan of salvation advocated in the New Testament. We speculate about what might be the case with persons who have never heard the Christian message, but we get no help from the New Testament. The church was given marching orders to take the gospel and so live as to demonstrate its saving power to the whole world. We are given no basis for guessing that people will be saved anyway, whether or not the church is faithful in its task.

The Christians, the representatives of the church, embody Christ in their lives. Their own lives witness to the power of the gospel. This is the plan of God for the ages.

So, when you and I consider God's will for our lives, we need to look briefly at this plan of God for the ages and note how our small lives fit into what God is doing throughout history.

When you and I have responsibility in a local church, such as serving on committees, teaching classes, working with children, or youth, or whatever, let us take very seriously what the church universal is and what a difference we can make in its work. We often think our decisions are in such small settings that it won't matter. But there is no one else! All of the rest are like you and me! They are no better and no worse. If we won't do it, why expect them to?

This is God's will—a plan and purpose for the ages.

# 9
# Providence—
# The Will of God in History

*As for you, you meant evil against me; but God meant it for good, to bring it about that many people should be kept alive, as they are today (Gen. 50:20).*

In trying to understand a biblical doctrine we need first to study the doctrine as it appears in the teachings of the Bible. This we have done, albeit briefly. Then, we need to see that doctrine in relationship to the other doctrines of faith.

The *will of God* is a very personal phrase. It is not limited to individual life; it includes our lives together. It is the purpose of God for you, me, and us. The larger term used in theology is the term, *providence.* The will of God is a very personal way of speaking about providence; but, providence is also personal.

The English word *providence* was formed from the Latin, *pro videre,* "to see before." The Greek antecedent or parallel is *pronoia,* "to know before."

In discussing the doctrine of God, theologians often try to speak of God's nature, or God as he is, and then, God in relationship to his creation. We maintain that God is Creator. Conceivably that could mean only that God made the universe, but what we know about God leads us to say something about God's continuing relationship with the universe. We call this continuing relationship between God and creation providence.

Theologians usually understand providence to include at least two elements: sustenance and governance. Sustenance means that God maintains and preserves the creation; governance means that God controls or guides it according to his purpose. Without God's sustenance, Augustine said the universe would collapse into nothingness. Without his governance or guidance it would plunge into chaos. Sometimes theologians use a third term *cooperation* or *working together* or *synergism* to indicate that area in which God's work and man's work overlap, intertwine, or work together. The word *concurrence* is also used.

Obviously, the most serious theoretical and practical problem we face is the problem of evil. How can we explain evil in the "good creation" of the "good and all-powerful" God? Satan is a created being who, like man, had fallen—a good being corrupted, for instance. Sinful men and women are good creations corrupted. Or, in the area of human freedom, some say that God is not the author of evil but "permits" it. Some say that God "permits evil" in order to achieve a greater good. Some use the idea of the "permissive will" of God. I find this term not only unhelpful but also objectionable for reasons stated elsewhere in this volume.

The doctrine of providence, however, is indispensable to biblical faith. It is almost synonymous with believing in God. Our grandparents regarded it as a precious belief for daily life. But, in our time we have overlooked it. Waldo Beach of the Divinity School of Duke University published an article in 1959 in which he pointed out that the doctrine of providence had become so unpopular and disreputable among contemporary theologians that they relegate it to the "museum of archaic curiosities."[1] Langdon Gilkey, professor of theology in the Divinity School of the University of Chicago has tried to reintroduce this doctrine into the theological curriculum, noting how it has been ignored. He followed his article of 1963, "The Concept of Providence in Contemporary Theology," with a book in 1976 entitled *Reaping the Whirlwind: A Christian Interpretation of History.* The published works on providence are relatively few in recent years; their dates say something about interest in the doctrine (see Bibliography).

## Biblical Teachings on Providence

*Abraham.* The Abraham narrative in Genesis (ch. 12 ff.) introduces the covenant in which God selected an individual man whose descendants would constitute a special covenant community. God would maintain a relationship with this people and bless them by guiding them toward a destiny. They were to be a pilgrim people who would ultimately convey to the other nations of the world the blessings of God. This theme is providence; God sustains and guides according to his purpose.

*Joseph.* We have already mentioned Joseph, but another word is needed. Jealous older brothers sold young Joseph into slavery. His unbelievable rise to power in Egypt is not merely a story of a home-town boy who did well. Rather, it is a narrative in which God guided and empowered Joseph to rise so as to be in a position to keep the covenant people alive. When the famine came to Israel, the older brothers went to Egypt to get grain and found themselves standing before Joseph. Joseph overcame his temptation to take revenge on them not due to a jovial disposition but because of a theological insight. He saw the guiding hand of God working to save him and his older brothers and their destiny.

The awareness that the God of all creation has a purpose for one makes it possible for that person to forgive. So Joseph, under God's providence, forgave and sustained the family. They had intended evil, but God had worked through their tangled history and had achieved his purpose. This is the idea of providence.

*The Exodus.* God did a "mighty act" when he delivered the Israelites from slavery in Egypt. Moses should have perished in the Nile, but he was rescued and rose to power. The Hebrews had no chariots, the jets and tanks of the ancient world; the Egyptians had many. The Hebrews should have lost their bid for freedom and remained slaves, but God sustained, governed, and delivered them. This is providence.

*Prophets.* Along with these "mighty acts," God raised up prophets, spokesmen whom he inspired to see what he was doing. They interpreted God's acts and words. Gerhard von Rad speaks of these prophets as charismatic leaders. Throughout Israel's history they called the people to remember what God had done and said to them in these revelatory events. This is the fabric of providence.

*Isaiah.* The prophets saw not only God's hand in Israel's history but also in the history of other nations. When Israel forgot God, got into a war and suffered, the prophets saw the enemy nations as scourges of God giving Israel what she deserved (Isa. 9:10-11; 10:5-11). The prophets did not mean that these pagan nations were consciously serving God, certainly not in a direct or willing sense; they were cruel, ambitious, aggressive kings just doing what such leaders did then and do now. But God was sovereign above them.

*Jeremiah.* Jeremiah saw God's providence in the life of the nation also. In the vision of the potter's wheel, God revealed to Jeremiah how the nations were as clay in the shaping hand of a potter. God shaped the vessel; but when the clay was marred, he shaped another vessel according to his pleasure. The potter could also destroy a vessel. God's providence included not only Israel and Judah but also pagan nations. The figure of the potter appears also in the New Testament (Rom. 9:21).

Jeremiah's view of providence is also very personal. He wrote about God's call, "Now the word of the Lord came to me saying, 'Before I formed you in the womb I knew you,/and before you were born I consecrated you;/I appointed you a prophet to the nations'" (Jer. 1:4-5).

*Psalms.* The hymn writers of Israel recognized God's providence not only in the affairs of men and nations but also in the world we call "nature." God's voice breaks the cedars of Lebanon (29:5) and rules over the flood (29:10). God was involved in people's history (95). All parts of creation, including plants and animals, heavenly bodies, light and darkness, are evidences of God's providential care (104).

*Job.* The wisdom writer wrestled with the problem of human suffering, always a part of the discussion of providence. Scholars cannot agree precisely on Job's solution to the problem; some think he intended to show that there was no "solution" in the human, rational sense. It is clear that he was trying to refute the age-old, die-hard idea that human prosperity and adversity are sure and direct indicators of God's favor and disfavor. Even though Job was the most righteous man of his age, he suffered the most. Suffering is not always the judgment of God on an individual's sin. The restoration of his family and property at the end are very difficult to interpret since it tends to reaffirm the notion the author was trying to correct.

But, in Job, Satan appears as a kind of prosecutor in the court of God; he is certainly not a superhuman rival of God. He is unable to get at Job until he cleared it with Yahweh. The author clearly preserved the ultimate sovereignty of God. God has no rivals; his realm is not in jeopardy.

Job's presentation of Satan is probably the basis for the later idea of the permissive will of God. If the book of Job is understood as literal history, then of course, there is no other alternative. If, however, the book of Job is a drama in which the inspired writer portrays his message, then there are other ways of understanding. The message, then, has to do with the mystery of the problem of suffering in a world created by God who is good. The mystery of suffering is not explained; it remains. God is faithful and the only one worthy of trust. God cares. But evil is real. Man's destiny is ultimately in the hands of God. If we trust God, we are not at the ultimate mercy of other forces. Suffering is temporal; God is ultimate. This is an important expression of providence even though we are left with many unanswered questions.

*Jesus.* In a previous chapter, we looked at Jesus' teaching on the will of God, so we can be brief here. God cares for the sparrows, the lilies, the grass; he cares even more for us (Matt. 10:26-33; 6:25-34). Jesus objected to many popular interpretations about sufferings and the judgment of God: the tragedy when the tower of Siloam collapsed killing eighteen people; Pilate's massacre of the Galileans (Luke 13:1-5); and the man born blind (John 9). Jesus refused to "explain," but he pointed to God's intent to save and forgive those who repent. We must urgently go to our human tasks of calling people to repentance and salvation.

*Paul.* Paul could teach more fully on the theme of providence because he came after the revelation of God in Jesus Christ. He saw the providential hand of God in his own life in that God called him from his mother's womb (Gal. 1:15). God had sustained him even while he was an enemy of the church. To Paul, God's providence also included the grand sweep of human history. In what may have been his earliest letter preserved in the New Testament, he wrote, "But when the time had fully come, God sent forth his Son, born of woman, born under the law, to redeem those who were under the law, so that we might receive adoption as sons" (Gal. 4:4-5). This statement reflects Paul's understanding that God who had been working in the events of the past, particularly those in the Old Testament, had now confronted his world with the revelation of his Son, who had come to redeem. One can hardly think of a more forceful statement of God's providence.

The great christological passages also portray the theme of providence. "In Christ God was reconciling the world to himself" (2 Cor. 5:19). "For in him all the fulness of God was pleased to dwell, and through him to reconcile to himself all things, whether on earth or in heaven, making peace by the blood of his cross" (Col. 1:19-20). Consider also Philippians 2:5-11. Note that in every instance God reveals himself to reconcile us to God—to save us. This is providence.

The doctrine of providence is stated clearly in many other New Testament passages but space will not permit a full discussion. Let's take one glimpse at a strange but wonderful book.

*The Apocalypse of John.* The last book of the New Testament is quite different from all the rest, but it speaks the Christian hope very clearly in the foreign language of apocalyptic. Read it again; read it quickly; don't stop to consider the ornate scenery and unidentified messengers who stand in the background; watch the drama. God is the sovereign Lord who brings it all to its desired goal. Jesus Christ is the Lamb who suffered a sacrificial death but becomes Lord of all. The faithful Christians, then undergoing persecution, obediently follow the Lamb through unbelievable sufferings to ultimate and eternal victory in the presence of God. The theme of providence stands out even in the strange apocalyptic imagery.

### Historical Interpretations of Providence

In order to understand a doctrine of the faith, we need to review how our predecessors understood the belief. Usually the theologians or thinkers of the church have told us how the Christians of their ages interpreted the faith. It is very interesting how each age reinterprets the faith in terms of its own attitudes or view of reality.

*Nonbiblical Parallels.* The doctrine of providence is really a biblical idea grounded in the biblical view of God the creator. Some similar ideas appear elsewhere, but upon examination we find that they are quite different from the biblical providence.

In Greek philosophy we encounter an idea which could easily be confused with providence. Stoicism comes closer to the Christian view than any other. Platonism had spoken of an all-inclusive and all-determining *pronoia,* "foreknowledge." This was a kind of world reason which gave meaning to the universe.

Aristotle had perceived the order and unity in the universe and suggested it implied control. The Stoics developed the idea of control or direction; this is close to providence.

The Stoic idea differed, however, from the biblical view. The biblical view grew out of a belief in God who created the world and revealed himself; it is God-centered, theological. The Stoic view was a kind of impersonal principle, not related to God. It was deterministic; it just works this way. The biblical view always includes human freedom; God pursues his purpose for creation but does not negate human freedom.

Stoicism would be only a "general providence" without the personal dimension. Biblical providence is both general and special. Special providence extends beyond the grand sweep of history to the specific individual person and his role in the will of God.

Another major difference is that while Stoicism knows of direction and unity, it does not know hope. The biblical view is permeated by an eschatological hope—a victory in the future.

*A Nonbiblical Rival—Fate.* The Stoic view presented a determinism. Greek drama often presented this view of human life as determined by the gods—fixed for us—*fate.* Human beings were at the mercy, or caprice, of the gods; they lived out what the gods had decreed. How different from biblical providence!

The Islamic religion also confronts the world with a determinism, fatalism if you will, expressed in the oft-used, "If Allah wills." Many Christians unknowingly have adopted this Islamic fatalism and use the phrase, "If God wills," in a similar way. In American folk-religion it is commonplace to encounter people who shrug off life's greatest injustices and even crimes by saying, "Well, God willed it," or, "If it wasn't God's will, it wouldn't have happened." Even a song can be popular on the theme, "Whatever will be will be." This is not providence; it is fate.

Fate breeds gloom and allows speech about chance and fortune. So, life may be either monolithically determined or meaningless. Christian providence is not fate.

*Augustine.* Augustine (AD 354-430) was the first great theologian of the Christian church to deal significantly with the theme of providence. Only Calvin has surpassed Augustine in terms of influence in teaching this doctrine, and Calvin built on the foundation of Augustine.

Augustine was born in AD 354, converted to Christianity in 386, ordained a priest in 391, a bishop in 395, and lived until 430. In several of his writings, *The Confessions, The City of God,* and *On Free Will,* he dealt with providence. In the year of his conversion, Augustine wrote "Divine Providence and the Problem of Evil." But let us look at this teaching on providence in *The Confessions.* This title designates the doctrines we "confess."

Augustine looked back, as Jeremiah and Paul had done, and saw the working of God in his life even while he was a fugitive from God. He had left the Manichaeans not because of his piety or theology but in order to pursue his study of astronomy. Yet, he could later see that he had been led in this move. His pious mother Monnica would have kept him in Carthage so she could seek to convert him to the true faith, but he lied and went to Rome. He went to Rome to enhance his own career. In Rome he could secure more apt students and become a greater teacher. He had no religious interest in going to Rome.

Later, Augustine went to Milan to hear the eloquent Ambrose preach. Augustine was a teacher of rhetoric; he was not interested in "what" Ambrose preached, only in "how." He wanted to improve his own rhetoric. The preaching of Ambrose, however, guided by the Holy Spirit, penetrated the heart of Augustine, and he became a Christian. Then, he understood how God had been working in his life even during his own unbelief and selfishness. He wrote about hearing Ambrose in his *Confessions,* "to him was I unknowingly led by thee that by him I might knowingly be led to thee."[2]

Augustine rejected chance and fate. Having used the word *fortune* earlier, he later apologized for it. To Augustine, God ruled over both the good and the evil as an all-wise sovereign. But Augustine held man responsible for his own sin. God ruled history through the free activity of men and women—not against it. Even though man's freedom may be restricted by sin, man is not coerced by God. God established order and harmony in the world; he sustains the powers of nature. Man's free will is one of those natures which God sustains. It is in this connection that Augustine stated his idea of God permitting evil.

He reasoned that if God sustained "natures" and one "nature" is our freedom, then God sustains us even when we are sinning. Consequently, he said that God permits evil and foreknows it. Augustine did not believe that God directly ordained evil.

*Aquinas.* Thomas Aquinas (1225-1274) was one of the most famous of the medieval theologians. He emphasized the principle of causality in dealing with providence. He used the words *Concursus Divinus* or "divine concurrence" in speaking of providence. God is the first cause, and "natural" causes are secondary causes. God, as first efficient cause, exercises pressure on secondary causes. However, the idea of causality, which is at home in nature and physics, is under a very heavy burden when used in speaking about the acts of a personal God.

In secondary causes we get to the problem of evil. Therefore, to Aquinas the world is interwoven with good and evil. Evil is so much a part of reality that it cannot be removed without destroying the good. So, he taught that God permits evil so that he could bring to reality a greater good.[3]

*John Calvin.* Calvin (1509-1564) has had more influence on the doctrine of providence in Protestantism than any other theologian. In the earlier editions of *The Institutes* (1539), his systematic writing on theology, he treated providence and predestination in the same chapter. In his last edition of *The Institutes,* however, he separated these subjects. He wrote on providence in Book One, chapter 16 and predestination in Book Three, chapters 21—24 along with his doctrine of the Holy Spirit.

Calvin's obsession with the sovereignty of God hardly left room for the freedom of man portrayed in the Scriptures. In the chapter, "God by His Power Nourishes and Maintains the World Created by Him, and Rules Its Several Parts by His Providence," he joined creation and providence inseparably. He argued that if providence does not mean that God exercises complete power over and control of the universe, then God was only a "momentary creator." So, the term *providence* required that God be the "everlasting governor and preserver" and that he "sustains, nourishes, and cares for everything he has made even to the least sparrow."[4] Calvin rejected any chance or fortune. He saw providence as the direct and daily operation of the universe. He allowed no freedom for the universe to follow its own pattern. For instance, he cited the battle of Joshua (Josh. 10:13) when the sun stood still to lengthen the day and the turning back of the sundial for Hezekiah (2 Kings 20:11; Isa. 38). Calvin said that these miracles prove that the sun does not rise and set daily by blind instinct of nature but that God himself did these chores daily to remind us of his heavenly favor.

He had no room for nature to have any independence even though it appears to have some. For instance, he argued, "some mothers have full and abundant breasts but others are almost dry, as God wills to feed one more liberally, but another more meagerly."[5] If Calvin was right in this illustration, modern people with baby formulas have overruled God and decreed that babies of mothers with barren breasts shall be well nourished too.

Calvin thought God determined all events. For instance, he told the story of a merchant who entered the woods with a company of faithful men. Unwisely, the merchant wandered away from his companions and fell among thieves, who killed him. Calvin said that God had not only "foreseen" that event but also had determined it by his decree. Calvin argued that it is not said that he foresaw the life of each man and saw how long a life would extend but that he determined and fixed the bounds that men cannot pass.[6]

Note how literalism distorts the meaning of Job. Note also how Calvin's dominant idea of God's total sovereignty leaves no room for human freedom, even though Calvin said that it did. Calvin insisted that he rejected fatalism, but did he?

One of the better emphases of Calvin is that kind of providence in which God's rule by the Holy Spirit is known in the church and in human lives.

*The Idea of Progress.* The idea of inevitable progress blossomed in the friendly environment of biological evolution and liberal theology. The period of fifty years preceding 1925 was an optimistic era. Biological evolution had advanced the notion of inevitable progress among plants and animals. The idea of inevitable progress caught on quickly in sociology and theology. People thought humanity was getting better: *Give us time and the twentieth century will be "The Christian Century." The kingdom of God will be on earth because we will build it.* This escalator failed us in the twentieth century. Two World Wars and all of the other atrocities killed this notion. Liberalism fell with it. The blossom perished leaving neither root nor stem.

I mention this idea which was influential in liberal theology because it says something about providence indirectly. If you neglect the biblical doctrine of providence, some substitute grows up in its place. Is there an element in human nature which requires this hope or expectation? Is it a part of reality? Is it an evidence of God the Creator?

*Futuristic Theology.* Along with and shortly after radical theology had its day, with its "secular Christianity" and the "death of God," a new kind of theology emerged. It is futuristic theology or "theology of hope." Two of the most famous theologians are Wolfhart Pannenberg and Jürgen Moltmann. They see the element of hope as the dominant force in Christian thought. The future becomes the power that draws the present into a more glorious future. These two differ significantly in a number of ways, and space will not permit a fuller discussion. But, again, this type of theology points out for us that humanity continues to come back to hope, expectation, or belief in the future. This belief is grounded in God.

In some way these ideas complement or derive from the biblical idea of providence. Life and the world do have meaning. Reality looks to the future for a fuller meaning or fulfillment. Is this not the idea of providence separated from its biblical setting and clothed differently?

We come back to the importance of the idea of providence—God continues to sustain and guide his creation toward its goal. This is the purpose of life—the purpose of the Creator. And this is what we mean when we speak of the "will of God" for our lives and his world.

# 10
# Warning—
# Popular Misconceptions of the Will of God

Those who go down to the sea in ships have a ringside seat for some of the most beautiful sights of nature. They observe the tranquil beauty of the calm ocean and its violent fury during the storm. They see a beauty in the moon and stars bathed by the endless stretches of the sea denied to those who look up only from the city. The whales, dolphins, and flying fish perform as if to entertain. The sailors learn to enjoy the ever-changing scenery and drama of the sea. But no sight at sea quite compares with that of a lighthouse which stands its lonely vigil on a barren reef or deserted promontory. The lighthouse flashes a double message: there is danger in these waters—shoals, rocks; but there is safety in the other direction. Anxious lookouts strain tired eyes searching the horizon for the lighthouses. Sleepy eyes can watch the flying fish.

In our journey we have already noted several common misunderstandings of the will of God. These are the more commonly known ways by which people miss the will of God. The listing of these dangers is intended to be a warning so we can move in another direction; others have suffered injury or shipwreck in these areas.

## Careless Theology

You may call it theology or doctrine, but it remains a vital part of sound Christian living. Right thinking is vitally related to right living. We have noted the Christian views of God, human existence, salvation, providence, and hope. Careless thinking about these and other doctrines may well lead to a misunderstanding of the will of God.

Theological reflection is a part of daily Christian life. We can

121

greatly increase our understanding of the doctrines of the Christian faith by study. Most churches feature such studies in their teaching curriculum. The sources of written materials are numerous. A reading plan should include doctrinal studies, ethical studies, biblical interpretation, and works which seek to relate faith to the issues of the contemporary world.

Careless theological thinking is a hindrance to the person who would know and do the will of God.

### The Mystery of Evil

There is no greater danger in our journey than the mystery of evil. It is a fact which threatens our existence in a theoretical as well as a practical way. Evil is an irrational thing which threatens our understanding of life.

A problem is something "there" waiting to be solved or overcome. A mystery, however, is something quite different. It defies a rational solution. It becomes a part of us; we are never done with it; we can't explain it. Perhaps we can come to terms with the mystery by settling for a victory over it.

Biblical faith offers no explanation of evil. It speaks of the fact and seriousness of evil and suggests several terms or concepts which help. The *fall* in Genesis 3 places the origin of human sin in human unbelief, pride, or disobedience. Adam and Eve did something that damaged their relationship with God. They exalted themselves above God, they disbelieved God, or they turned against God. This turning from God was followed immediately by numerous changes: alienation from God; expulsion from the garden; estrangement from the earth and each other; and a murder in the second generation. The early chapters of Genesis portray the tragic movement away from God to the Tower of Babel, a lasting expression of human pride.

The sin in Eden has become the sin of the whole race. And, we all know fallenness within ourselves. This contradiction which appears to have grown out of our misuse of God-given freedom is a part of us now. Locating it in the misuse of freedom, however, does not answer the question, Why?

Biblical faith portrays a tempter who suggested the sin against God. The biblical writers used several terms for the tempter or adversary. *Satan* appears three times in the Old Testament and many times in the New Testament. In the New Testament there are several other terms for this adversary, such as the *devil*. The author of Revelation identified the serpent as the dragon, the devil, and Satan. While the tempter appears to suggest that people turn against God, he is never the cause of their sin. People are held responsible for their actions. They are not at the mercy of this evil embodiment because with God's help they can be victorious. So, Satan does not explain our mystery of evil. The term *Satan* points toward it.

Some theologians have spoken of natural evil or evil resulting from physical nature. They speak of storms, earthquakes, diseases, and the like. It is becoming increasingly difficult to speak of nature as evil since by scientific technology we are learning to deal with some of these "so-called" natural evils. If they can be solved technologically, then we probably should not speak of them in a moral term, *evil*.

Reinhold Niebuhr located the mystery of evil in the human misuse of freedom and gave a clear analysis of it in his *Nature and Destiny of Man*. Edwin Lewis in his *Creator and Adversary* placed the adversary on a par with God. He saw this evil personage or power as eternal; life is an eternal struggle with evil; the outcome is not settled yet. Lewis has been called an out-and-out dualist or Zoroastrian, but he spent his adult life as a teacher of Christian theology.

We must not forget that evil is real. It is more than a problem; it is a mystery. And it threatens us.

The most devastating question facing the Christian theologian is this question: How can you explain the fact of such evil in the world if God is both good and powerful? The defense of this paradox is called theodicy.

Theologians from early times have struggled with this question. Obviously, we have some alternatives: God would remove evil if he could; God is able to but is not willing to do so; he is neither willing nor able to do so; he is both willing and able to do so.[1] Only the last option is acceptable to the Christian, but the mystery then becomes intensified, not removed.

The New Testament provides no explanation of the mystery; it does, however, provide victory. Jesus was tempted but overcame it. Jesus Christ won a victory over sin, death, and the devil. That victory comes to us as we believe in Christ. The book of Revelation portrays the struggle with and victory over evil in apocalyptic language. But it is victory, not explanation.

You have to be disappointed that I cannot deal more adequately with the problem of theodicy in this volume. But let me point out two significant and guiding ideas: the mystery of evil is a constant danger and is probably more serious than most of our statements about it; and, in Christ we can know a victory over evil.

So, the warning about evil becomes a hope or a promise. God promised to work with us as we do his will. He can lead us to victory over evil. And, this is his will!

## Whatever Will Be Will Be

People say it in times of defeat, sorrow, or frustration—not often in times of joy. It is the expression which signals resignation. They use it to comfort a friend or themselves. But it is inconsistent with their lives and beliefs. They are devoted sincere Christians. They work to do right and avoid wrong. They don't wait for good things to happen but try to make good things happen. And yet, without careful thinking, they voice with resignation, "Whatever will be will be."

Where did this alien belief come from? Did someone sneak it in inside a Trojan horse? It doesn't belong among Christians. It cuts the nerve of moral responsibility. It assumes an inevitability in human life or blames God for things which may be of human origin. It may lock the door to opportunity. Can you imagine Joseph as a sullen slave rotting in an Egyptian jail cell saying, "Whatever will be will be"? Can you imagine Paul in Troas voicing this resignation? No! Both persons looked for opportunity and turned defeat into achievement. We must not allow faith to degenerate into resignation nor hope into gloomy waiting. Faith is a confident commitment; hope is a joyful expectation. Apart from the miracles of God and his other acts hidden from us, "Whatever will be won't be" unless we or others do it. If we would know and do the will of God, we must stay out of this dead-end street. It leads nowhere!

### Everything Works Out for the Best

This is a more cheerful version of religious fatalism. If we are going to be lost on the journey there is something to be said for being lost with cheerful companions. But cheerfulness purchased at this price is a disappointing investment. It appears to have been encouraged by the translation of Romans 8:28 in the King James Version. It may have grown out of a genuinely cheerful outlook on life. The promises of God certainly provide a basis for hope—cheerful hope.

The general optimistic statement, however, that everything works out for the best denies human responsibility. It also rather blandly assumes that the providence of God will deflect or override all human evil. It overlooks the fact that human tragedies and wrongs are real. We live in the aftermath of incredibly savage wars which have caused untold injury and suffering to the human family. We prepare for another such war while skirmishing on several potentially disastrous battlefields. We don't want our officials to assume casually that everything works out for the best. We know that it has not always done so in the past. And, we want them to exhaust every possible effort to see that it works out acceptably this time.

Biblical faith does not encourage gullible, unthinking optimism. It acknowledges that we people are sinners and capable of unbelievable cruelty. It also gives us a basis for hope in God. We can pray to him, believing. Knowing that everything does not always work out for the best, we can work harder or in a different direction. We cannot know and do the will of God acceptably if we subscribe to the popular notion, "It will all work out."

## The Permissive Will of God

This phrase has a long and illustrious history. Theologians like Augustine found some help in it. Others have found it inspiring in that, "God permits evil in order to accomplish a greater good." Biblical writers often spoke so as to leave the impression that God not only permitted but perhaps even sent evil.

Leslie D. Weatherhead allowed the permissive will of God while he distinguished among "God's intentional will," his "circumstantial will" and his "ultimate will." People who use these terms are obviously dealing with the fact that out of suffering or evil, God can and does achieve some good purpose. They may also be defending the reputation of God by not saying he "caused" it.

To go against such an array of evidence and thinkers may appear to be a losing proposition. Perhaps, I am reacting to a legal use of the word, *permit*. If a passerby observes small children playing with a dangerous explosive which they do not recognize, he has a moral obligation to intervene. If he does not and the children are killed or injured, there are legal as well as moral obligations. It is said of him that he did not *cause* the accident but *permitted* it. In this context, *permitted* means: the children were irresponsible; the man was in a position to intervene, and everyone would have approved his intervention.

When we say, "God permits evil or suffering," the context is different. We are not irresponsible children, but very responsible persons. God's intervention might well violate the sacred trust he has given us. The situation is not the same.

The "permitting" is brought into the situation at the wrong place. God permits, rather gives freedom. In our freedom, we do the things that are evil or appear to be so. God forbids us to do evil. The biblical teachings on responsibility stress this. It would be better not to say that God permits us to do wrong or suffer wrong.

The wrath of God in Romans means that *"God* gave them up in the lusts of their hearts" (1:24). This does not really mean that God permitted them to do this; he had tried everything else to get them to do right and they had refused. In the last resort, he merely "gave them up." Giving them up does not mean permitting. It means they don't act with God's approval.

Of course, we all know many experiences in which God worked for our good in spite of evil and suffering encountered on the way. It seems better to me to avoid this popular interpretation of the will of God.

### Blessings in Disguise

This popular idea is similar to the preceding one. People often tend to reinterpret unpleasant experiences from which they learned something of value as God's way of teaching them. The seeming defeat or disappointment was really a "blessing in disguise." This may be another wording for the idea that "everything works out for the best." It may be a comfort in some defeats of life, but it may be a pitfall in others. And, worse than that, it may be untrue.

A young man once sought my counsel about his desire to enter the Christian ministry. He talked for a long time about his troubles in the university. He disguised his failures, probation, and removal from the university as God's way of telling him to enter the seminary. I had to probe him to get the truth. If he had told me he had failed because of inner turmoil about a life's vocation, I could have understood it. Other persons had conspired with him to interpret his failure as God's way of speaking. He was really hurt when I told him that failure in a university is a poor way to get into seminary and that such mental dishonesty would disqualify him if he got there. Someone had told him that God was speaking to him in his situation. That may be so, but I would suspect that what God said first would be closer to the Dean's statements than to the student's.

A man was injured in an accident and could no longer engage in athletics. He became a scholar. Later, he said about his physical injury, "It was the best thing that ever happened to me." Now, this is not clear thinking. God gave us our physical health and abilities. It is a tragedy when we lose any of our faculties. A better way is to thank God that with his help and the support of others we can utilize those God-given talents remaining in order to achieve a meaningful life. It is "God working with us for good" even in a tragic situation.

When death comes into a home and claims a loved one prematurely, there are those kind persons who say, "It is really a blessing. God knows best." That interpretation, despite the love of the one speaking, leaves much to be desired. I hope the surgeons, nurses, and pharmacists agree with my approach and go about their important tasks with some idea of what is at stake in what they do. Parents who lose a child can survive the loss and go on living. If they believe in God and have Christian friends, they can overcome. But don't tell them the loss of their child is a blessing in disguise. They know better than you do about that. Children cannot be replaced. Others can be born, but the dead child cannot be replaced. You cannot replace the playful laughter and joyful smile of that particular child. At night after such a loss, a parent sleepily walks into an empty bedroom to check the covers on a baby bed only to awaken fully beside a crib that is now empty. In the following years, these parents may have a depth of understanding and sympathy for others, but don't call their loss a blessing. God's grace is the blessing; the loss of a child is a tragedy.

### Rationalizing God's Will

Since we are rational beings, we interpret our experiences and try to fit them together into a meaningful whole. It is necessary that we do this, and great benefits accrue if we do it honestly. The football team meets on Monday to look at the films of the game played the previous day. Under the watchful interpretation of the coaches, the players learn what they did right and what they did wrong. It is a time for honesty.

In matters of personal living, there is a subtle temptation to interpret our lives in terms of the values and motivations we cherish. One meaning of the verb *rationalize* is, "to make conformable to principles satisfactory to reason." Or, rationalizing is often an exercise of interpreting our experiences in a way that makes them fit into our purpose whether or not the interpretation is entirely factual. This is particularly the case with our failures.

Occasionally, we encounter a person who rationalizes the will of God into one of his failures. A seminary student from a very conservative background applied to an Eastern graduate school for admission to work toward a doctorate in theology. He failed the entrance tests and was not admitted. Later, he explained to his friends that before applying he had heard that the school had a rather liberal outlook. He had prayed that if it was not God's will for him to go there, he would not be admitted. His failure, therefore, had been God's will. He felt good about it. A secular coach would expect more honesty from his players about a failure in a football game.

The doctors, nurses, and other members of the hospital staff had done all that they could do, but a life slipped away. Grief-stricken people said, "The Lord knew best. The Lord's will be done." Does this mean that the medical people had been working against God's will? Many of them believe that they are working with God's will when they attempt to heal people. When they fail, for whatever reasons, they grieve too.

It may be much more faithful to God for us to acknowledge that we failed, were defeated, or just didn't know any more to do. Why rearrange the facts to support a religious belief, such as a previous understanding of the will of God?

## Applying Individual Interpretations to Others

We do interpret our experiences in relationship to the whole of life. Some of our interpretations are purely personal—like believing God preserved my life in a plane accident at sea. The danger comes when I apply my interpretation to others or try to make a universal truth out of it. Mother prayed for her four sons in World War II; all four came home safely. She believed God answered her prayers and thanked him. She had to be careful, however, in telling of his hearing her prayers because many of her neighbors had sons for whom they prayed who did not return.

## Forgetting the Context

The will of God to us is a theological conviction, and it has to do with life. We speak about the will of God in a context of theological beliefs; it has its meaning there. A word of caution may be appropriate about interpreting God's will too readily in other contexts.

A man had enjoyed a good week speculating on the stock market. He remarked, "God has been very good to me this week." Then he told of his profits. The age-old belief that prosperity signals God's favor and adversity signals his disfavor continues to live. Job tried to correct it, but the belief lives on. Do you think God works in the stock market?

The investor needs to know the stock market or follow the advice of those who do. Perhaps I have missed something. We have a difficult time now persuading people to believe in God. (He keeps company with questionable people and has had bad press in our time.) If they get the notion that their losses on the stock market are related to God's role in it . . . ?

## Explaining the Unexplainable

We have noted some questions Jesus refused to answer or at least, he refused to explain. There are many questions for which we have no answers. In our limited knowledge, we don't even know how to ask some of the questions. Every Christian should be able to answer self or others with a gracious, "I don't know," when that is the case.

Some of us who entered the Christian ministry when we were quite young made the mistake of not admitting our limited knowledge. We felt it so threatening to admit our limited knowledge that we gave explanations for the most difficult and mysterious questions and situations. But, as we grew toward maturity in the faith, we learned that we know and serve God even with limited knowledge and maintain our integrity even when we don't know all the answers.

Some of the illustrations above represent the immature notion that we have to explain everything—and sometimes in terms of the will of God.

## Obsession with "My Will"

Some interpreters of our age think we have been too interested with ourselves. They use such terms as *Meism*. An inordinate concern with one's self is childish and sinful. The mature person learns to look out beyond self to others and even learns to have a sense of humor about oneself. Of course, I have a will. It is me. But I find my place among all the others.

We have all heard the old quip about the person in the stands who was so concerned with self that when the football team huddled on the field, he thought they were talking about him. It is not too unusual to meet a Christian who thinks that the rain which spoiled the picnic was the result of a conspiracy in heaven focused on one picnic. Failure in business often results from economic and political factors which were years in forming. Every person in this world is in danger of these powers which are often unpredictable.

We certainly should not take ourselves so seriously in these matters. If we fail in our work, it is not the end of the world. If my plans for life are thwarted by a new draft law followed by military service at a most inconvenient time, it is not the end. The will of God has to do with his purpose and our living for him. We can do that quite acceptably in many different sets of circumstances. To be sure, I should have my plans, and I have adequate reason for resentment if bungling in government leads to the necessity for a new draft law. But, I can know a real and genuine purpose in life, the will of God, even though I don't get to do it my way, in my place, or according to my plans. "Thy will be done!"

# 11
# The Way—
# Knowing and Doing the Will of God

*Do not be conformed to this world but be transformed by the* renewal of your mind, *that you may prove what is the will of God, what is good and acceptable and perfect (Rom. 12:2, author's italics).*

*Not in the way of eye service, as men-pleasers, but as servants of Christ,* doing the will of God from the heart *(Eph. 6:6, author's italics).*

It is time for us to close. I thought of entitling this session a "Conclusion" but that would suggest an end, and we are really talking about a beginning. I thought of using the term "The Answer," but that would suggest that we had begun with a question or a problem and had now solved it. I thought about "Victory"; indeed, it would be a victory if we follow the will of God, but it is hardly a victory unless we do so. Let us speak of "The Way" since we are on a pilgrimage. By "The Way," we mean the route we travel as we attempt to know and do the will of God.

We have focused primarily on the teachings of Scripture which deal with knowing and doing the will of God. Those teachings do not sum up a set of rules which could be applied in solving a problem. They do not constitute something like a road map that could be used mechanically on a journey. Rather, they deal with truths which go into the building of the Christian life, and undergird the person who seeks to live by the will of God. These guidelines become a part of people who in using their own minds come to decide what is the will of God.

Knowing and doing the will of God involves a discipline of study, reflection, and decision. Instead of a set of rules, we actually have some "essentials" that point the way. These essentials become convictions of faith and hence a part of the mind and heart process. Doing the will of God is a sacred act in living. It includes right thinking but goes beyond thought to action born of a right heart. I cannot divide any specific instance into mind and heart. These always come together as companions. The careful understanding of the mind guides the heart. The purity of the heart may even correct the mind, but it incorporates understanding into convictions of life. To do the will of God we must have clear minds and pure hearts.

Obedience in Christian practice is an act of a clear mind and a pure heart. To do something merely because the mind recognizes it to be in keeping with the law of God is compliance—not obedience. This leads to legalism. To do something because the heart dictates it without the agreement of the mind is to be divided. That would be like the person who climbed the church steeple and then kicked the ladder down. He couldn't tell someone else how to get up there with him, neither could he get down by himself. Obedience joins mind and heart together or grows out of a united mind and heart. We do the will of God joyfully because we are convinced that it is right and good.

Our study has frequently pointed out that the individual knows and does the will of God within the community of persons. Any talk about the individual without the community leads to error; likewise, any talk about the will of God within the community which neglects the individual leads to error. Our lives, and I understand our lives to be gifts from God, are always and at the same time individual and corporate. We cannot look at the subheadings which follow as either "individual" or "community" in nature; they are always both. Even Bible study, though undertaken individually, involves the community. Community and individuality are always together as we seek to understand and do God's will. In the following pages, I am assuming the individual to be in a community relationship.

Let us look at the essentials for recognizing the way to know and do the will of God as individuals in community on the Christian pilgrimage.

## Know Your Beliefs

Doctrinal beliefs are more than intellectual statements; they are the convictions of faith and life. They are the navigational stars for our journey. They guide us on the way. Failure to follow sound theology is the sure way to lose sight of the will of God.

An earlier chapter focused on the Christian understanding of God, human life, salvation, providence, and hope. These major doctrines and many others constitute the fiber of faith. They undergird us with strength; they guide us aright.

Our study has insisted that we look upon the will of God as the personal purpose God has for each of us. God is the Father of our Lord Jesus Christ. As such, he is like the shepherd who looked for the lost sheep. He is like the woman who looked for the lost coin. He is like the father who waited for and forgave the lost son. God, in Christian faith, revealed himself in Jesus Christ. Our view of God is always Christ-centered. If you want to know more about God, go to Jesus Christ.

If God is our heavenly Father, what bearing does that have upon my decision about a lifework? Many people are concerned about the will of God for their work in life. We have noted that God has called us to himself and that he has given us a wondrous freedom. Some persons believe God has called them to certain ministries in the church; others do not. But these others are called to be Christians. That is a life calling. Now, how will you earn your living? That is up to you. God has given you freedom. You have talents, things you love to do, things you are good at doing. The community has needs which you and I can recognize. Choose something in keeping with your talents and the good of the human family and enjoy doing it. Don't you think your heavenly Father can get in touch with you if he has something "special" in mind? Trust God! Use the talents and opportunities you have! That is doing the will of God. Of course, prayer to God and consultation with others are always appropriate in making decisions such as this one.

## Know Your Bible

In our study, we have looked primarily at the teachings of Jesus and Paul, with some attention to other teachings in Scripture. The Bible is a treasure, a storehouse of treasure, in terms of information and inspiration for every part of the Christian life, especially for knowing and doing the will of God.

The Bible is the textbook of the church and the Christian life. The Holy Spirit is God with us. To be sure, the Holy Spirit guides us. We know his guidance most often as he illuminates our minds to grasp the word from God as we study the Scriptures. The Bible should not be seen as a competitor with the church or Holy Spirit. The church, the Holy Spirit, and Scripture are constant companions; they complement each other.

The Bible is authoritative because God revealed himself in those events recorded in Scripture and inspired his chosen witnesses, prophets, and apostles to hear and record his Word. They were indeed "men moved by the Holy Spirit" and they "spoke from God" (2 Pet. 1:21). We should read the Bible devotionally. We should also study it diligently.

One can grasp the essential meaning of Scripture even without formal study in a Bible school or seminary. If one has two good translations, an English dictionary, and a one-volume commentary, he can do responsible study and interpretation of the Bible. It would be wise to study the Gospels and Epistles (letters) first. Leave Revelation for the position it has in the canon—last. You can know your Bible if you are willing to study it.

A concordance is a helpful tool for Bible study, but it won't direct you to a biblical passage which will give you a quick read-out on the will of God. Your and my situation is not usually specifically discussed in the Bible. We have to study the Bible systematically and learn its truths. Then, when we have to decide a question about God's will for our lives, we have the biblical knowledge we need.

## Prayer and Worship

Prayer is conversation with God, communion. Prayer may focus on adoration, intercession, thanksgiving, or petition. Sometimes we pray just to be in God's presence. In prayer, we speak to God; we also listen. It usually takes more time and effort to listen than to speak.

Knowing the will of God is a legitimate subject for prayer. Strength and guidance in doing the will of God is an answer to prayer. But we shouldn't rush into God's presence with a panic prayer about his will until we have done our "homework." We should not tie up the communication lines until we have decided what we want to talk to God about, how we understand the situation, others who are involved, and so forth. You would not go into the presence of any other person to seek guidance or approval without preparing your case. And another word of caution is appropriate. Don't enter the conversation of prayer with God until you have the time and are willing to listen.

We have many assurances that God wants us to approach him in prayer about our concerns in life. We certainly have confidence in his vital interest in his will for our lives. We should pray for his guidance and be prepared to receive it in whatever way he chooses to make it known.

Worship is also private and public. We enter God's presence and wait. He makes himself known as he wills. We adore him, praise him, hear his Word, are convicted of our sins, receive his forgiveness, intercede for others, rejoice, and go to serve. Worship cleanses the soul; it also cleanses the atmosphere so we can see our navigational stars. In the sacred communion of worship, the will of God makes sense. It ties mind and heart together.

Again, a word of encouragement which may sound like a caution. If you have not spent much time in worship lately, don't expect to rush into church for a quick answer about the will of God for your life. There is a special language involved in communion with God. It does involve a time of learning from and with those who already know the language. The language barrier can be overcome only by participation in worship with others who already speak with God. My word is an encouragement. If you will worship, God will make his will known to you.

## Converse with the Church

The Bible is the primary source of our information about God and his ways—his will. The church is a very helpful source also. In the study of theology, the church is a secondary source; in the Christian life there is nothing "secondary" about the church.

The church, as in Ephesians, is the whole body of Christ. We participate in the life of the church with Paul, Augustine, Luther, and Carey. Our participation is known most clearly through our involvement in local churches. In this fellowship of the church we learn and do the will of God. Others doing the will of God help us clarify our own views. They also give us encouragement and strength. One cannot really do the will of God apart from the fellowship of other believers.

But through reading church history we can hold conversation with the church of the ages. If we would know the will of God, we need the counsel of our Christian predecessors like Augustine, Calvin, and Luther.

## Conversation with Others

Every Christian should be in regular conversation with other serious believers. We walk in pilgrimage with them. They see us more clearly than we see ourselves sometimes. My friend Ed Bratcher of Virginia has been one of my most helpful advisers since seminary days. He knows me, likes me well enough to desire the best for me, but is not an admirer to the degree of giving appraisals that are too optimistic. He tells me the truth even though it is not always cushioned with compliments. I think the words which describe this attitude is "Christian love."

Serious conversation with other serious Christians is an essential for those who would do the will of God. We grow stronger individually as we enter an interdependent relationship with like-minded, committed Christians.

## Know Your World

The only context in which we can do the will of God is this world and this age. It has a past and a present; whether the world will have a future depends partially on whether we do God's will. We need to know it. Of course, our knowledge is limited, but we can raise the limits.

God's purpose does include the world. History does have meaning to Christians. God's redemptive work is a grand purpose for his creation. This is why Jesus spoke, "Thy will be done, on earth as it is in heaven" (Matt. 6:10).

Our understanding of the will of God for us involves this purpose of God for this world and the ages. "My will" may be an expression of the old self-centeredness we encountered as sin. My salvation may be secured in that turning from "my will" to "thy will." The context in which we do God's will involves this world and this age.

## Know Your Own Immediate Situation

The total context gives perspective and grand purpose; but we are right here in a limited situation. We have to understand the will of God for us in these limitations. The past through which we have come is out of reach, except through memory and study of history; our future is uncertain; complaining and blaming others won't help us. Some doors are open; others are closed. We must make our decisions and act now. The night cometh!

While I was working on this manuscript, I learned that my former pastor and friend was ill. He and I had camped and fished together in remote regions of Ontario and Northern Manitoba. When I went to see him in the hospital, I learned that he had a cancerous tumor which had already spread into three organs of his body. What is the will of God for a person who is terminally ill? My friend continued to hope. He arranged for another minister to care for his congregation. He made business decisions for his family. He prayed and worshiped God. For several weeks his ministry was to his family, a few close friends, hospital personnel, and to his church through reports of others. He remained a Christian man, a devoted husband, a caring pastor, a sportsman in conversation, and a friend until two days after Christmas when he died. In his situation, the options were few. But he gave evidence of being in the will of God until the end.

The will of God in my situation involves whatever opportunities I have. A young physician had recently arrived on his mission field with great plans and hopes. A war started. He didn't cause it, didn't want it, thought it was totally evil, but he was caught in it. Now, what shall he do? This doctor was still the same person with the professional skills to heal and save lives, and the situation called for it. The will of God appeared to be to use his skills in the new situation and do what he could for the people involved.

Other questions are important. Who or what caused the war? What could have prevented it? These are questions for the historians. The immediate question about the will of God involves our response to the present situation. To be sure, we cannot be indifferent to the causes because we have a responsibility to try to prevent wars in the future. But the question is, What is God's will for me now?

One mark of emotional maturity is the ability to recognize and accept the true situation in life. When a person is terminally ill or caught in one of life's tragedies, the mature response is the acceptance of reality. The questions, Why? or Why me? yield no answers.

### Relate Thy Will, Our Will, and My Will

The will of God is the goal of life. It is Jesus' "thy will." God's will somehow summarizes "our will." God wills what is right for others. But there is "my will." My will is my own integrity. God does not want us to be subservient. Jesus was never stronger than when he determined with his will to do the will of the Father.

As creatures of God with wills of our own, we respond to God with intelligent listening and reflecting. Then, when we know God in Christ, we learn joyful obedience of both mind and heart.

God wants no grudging surrender of our wills. Like an earthly father who is wise, God wills that his children do right because they have decided with their own wills what is right. It is not enough to comply in surrender to sheer authority. So, be faithful to your own will until you learn the will of God and see that it is best.

## Renew Your Commitment

Faith is commitment. The mind and heart combine in our commitment to God. The individual and the community are rightly related only in our commitment. All along we have noted this knowing by faith, knowing by involvement in the journey, knowing with all faculties of mind and heart. This knowing happens in Bible study, prayer, worship, living, and struggle. Commitment sets the course. Commitment keeps us on course. Keep your commitment "current."

## Leave an Opportunity Open for Providence

Paul taught us to look for the open doors of opportunity when other doors closed. He also taught us to make our plans and follow them when we can. Perhaps we need one other admonition: Leave a door open for providence so that God may enter our lives if he wills.

As we journey, others join us along the way. They bring new strength and purpose to our pilgrimage. We would never meet them unless we had already begun the journey. Some of them have become the personal expressions of providence in our lives. We need to leave our plans open enough for God in his providence to enter.

For reasons too numerous to narrate I decided to do my study for the ministry in The Southern Baptist Theological Seminary in Louisville, Kentucky. In that setting, I met many persons who have enriched my life as I have tried to do the will of God. One of them was a young professor, William H. Morton. In my graduate study, I became his assistant and later joined the faculty with him. We became friends. Our children grew up together. We worked together, took our vacations together, faced deep grief together, and shared the Christian life with each other. He has been an inspiration as well as a companion. It seems to me that God, in his providence, guided me to this friend. Do you think God may achieve his will in our lives sometimes by introducing us to these choice persons along the way?

My daughter, Anna Belle, chose to attend Northwestern University in Evanston, Illinois. She knew no one on that campus. Naturally, I had hoped she would attend one of our denomination's many fine colleges or universities on whose campuses I knew a number of people. She went to Northwestern. Her mother and I prayed for her. She went early to band camp to try out for the marching band. She met a number of exceedingly fine young people who became her friends. She was assigned to professors who were not only professionally outstanding but also personally interested in students. Is it all right to believe that God answers prayers of parents by guiding children into the company of other persons along the way?

We have to make decisions in life in the light of the information we have: What occupation should I choose? Whom should I marry? Where should I live? We make these decisions in the light of our information, purpose, and evaluations. We pray for guidance and allow room for God to enter if he wills.

God may call you to leave your lifework and enter a special full-time ministry. If so, you can have confidence in his will if you have faced the decision according to the essentials briefly pointed out in our study. But, don't think the call of God necessarily means for you to leave what you are doing to become a preacher or missionary. The call to do the will of God may mean for you to stay where you are, doing what you do and love best. Leave room for God's providence.

About four or five years ago George Powers enrolled as a student in the seminary in which I teach. He had spent twelve years in the United States Army and had reached the rank of major. He had begun what appeared to be an illustrious career. He believed that God had called him to be a chaplain in the army. A seminary degree was prerequisite, so he resigned from the army and came to the seminary. He became my advisee and friend. When he told me about his "call," I had some doubt that he could get back into the army. I knew that the Baptist quota was filled and that there was a waiting list of men without his seniority who would likely be given preference. I advised him to prepare to be a pastor in case the chaplaincy was closed to him. He worked diligently, served as a pastor while he was a student, and refused to give up hope.

To my surprise, he was appointed chaplain the the United States Army and retained his seniority. He wrote me on January 12, 1980, "the call we talked so much about has truly been confirmed for me. I know that I'm right where God wants me and where he prepared me to be over the years." George made his decision, took his risks, moved on to prepare, and is confident that he is doing God's will. George Powers is a clear example of a person who is confident of God's will in his life.

## When Doubts Obscure

In closing, I want to tell a story about my early understanding of the will of God. Perhaps it will help in times of doubt, when the way is not clear, but you must go on.

Earlier I told you that I interrupted my college years for military service. I had always had an interest in flying but had not had opportunity to learn how. The United States Navy was giving free lessons then so I enlisted as a flight student. After completing flight training and receiving my wings and commission, I was assigned to single-engine, carrier-type aircraft.

For a number of reasons, most of our flying was done in formations of aircraft—three, six, twelve, or eighteen in a group. In order to carry out the particular assignments it was necessary for the aircraft to be in close formation. It was much safer to fly close together with the wings slightly overlapping separated vertically by a few feet. Then the pilot could usually see a part of the other aircraft in the clouds and if one began to drift into the other plane it could be seen more quickly. The flight leader had to keep the airplanes in close formation in order to guide them through maneuvers. So, we flew very close together for effectiveness and for safety.

Formations cannot maneuver as easily as a single aircraft and we would sometimes be in the clouds for short distances. The visibility would be almost zero. Sometimes one could not see any part of the next plane. There was an uneasy feeling when the clouds were full of airplanes with fourteen-foot propellers turning eighteen hundred revolutions per minute.

We trimmed the aircraft control surfaces to remain in formation with the lead plane even with "hands off" the controls. We did this while we were in the clear. Then, when we entered the clouds the planes would maintain their relative positions for a reasonably short time even if we lost sight of the other planes in the clouds. The secret was to have the airplane on course and steady before entering the clouds. Then, when visibility was lost, we kept everything just like it was. No climbing, turning, or diving. No changes! Straight ahead. The undisciplined pilot was tempted to bolt. That would have led to certain disaster. The safest course: Go right on doing what you were doing.

On numerous occasions, I recall entering the clouds with eleven other airplanes behind me. After a few moments of tense waiting, we broke into the clear. I would look back to count them as they came out still in formation—all eleven of them came right out of the clouds. It worked!

Many times on my journey with the will of God I have not been able to see the way clearly. I was related to others, and we were on the way. We had set our course on the basis of convincing evidence when the skies were clear. Then, the doubts and uncertainties came. Remembering the lesson learned in my youth while flying formation, I tried to continue on course with those other lives and futures which were so closely related to my own. It takes more concentration and discipline and faith to go on in times of doubt, but it is more dangerous to bolt or hesitate.

Our mind takes over when the heart gets weak, next time your heart will provide the courage when the mind is fearful. If you have worked through the problem in times that are clear, you can go right on during the doubts and storms. There is a thrill to it.

In the light of what we know about the will of God and the pilgrimage, let us be on our way. We know there will be doubts and clouds ahead; other pilgrims have told us so. Let us set our course together and be sure we plan to stay in the right relationship to one another. Then, when the clouds obscure the way, let us go right on. We will all come through together. "I'll see you on the other side!"

# Notes

CHAPTER 1
1. This story has been told in various versions. I don't have the original version. H. G. Wood, "God's Providential Care and Continual Help—Romans vii.28," *Expository Times*, July 1958, p. 292 cited Wetstein as his source for a version which included a cock, a cat, and a lamp.

CHAPTER 2
1. Werner Georg Kümmel, *The Theology of the New Testament*, John Steely, trans. (Nashville: Abingdon Press, 1973), p. 53.
2. Rudolf Bultmann, *Theology of the New Testament*, Kendrick Grobel, trans. (New York: Charles Scribner's Sons, 1951), I, pp. 11-22.

CHAPTER 3
1. Ken Denlinger, "Stoneface," *The Kansas City Times*, December 25, 1979, p. 1F, quoting Tom Landry.

CHAPTER 4
1. C. H. Dodd, "The Epistle of Paul to the Romans," *The Moffatt New Testament Commentary* (New York: Harper and Brothers Publishers, 1932), pp. 137 ff.

CHAPTER 5
1. Anders Nygren, *Commentary on Romans* (Philadelphia: Muhlenberg Press, 1949), p. 416.

CHAPTER 7
1. I use the words *historical* and *historic* in the sense that *historical* designates that which merely happened; *historic* is an event or person which not only happened but also continues to influence history. The Declaration of Independence is both historical and historic. Jesus Christ is both.

CHAPTER 8
1. Waldo Beach, "The Pattern of Providence," *Theology Today*, July 1959, pp. 232-244.
2. Augustine, *Confessions* Book V. Ch. XIII.

3. Thomas Aquinas, *Summa Theological* 3; I, 3 and 3.

4. John Calvin, *Institutes of the Christian Religion*, Book I, Ch. XVI, 3.

5. Ibid, 1.

6. Ibid., 9 citing Job 14:5.

CHAPTER 10

1. Paul Schilling, *God and Human Anguish* (Nashville: Abingdon Press, 1977), p. 38 cites the classic framing of this question by Epicurus reported by Lactantius who died about AD 330.

# Bibliography

Allen, Cady H. *The Guidance of God*. Philadelphia: Westminster Press, 1968.

Aquinas, Thomas. *Treatise on God*. Tests selected and translated by James F. Anderson. Englewood Cliffs: Prentice-Hall, Inc., 1963.

Augustinus, Aurelius (Augustine). *Divine Providence and the Problem of Evil*. Translated by Robert P. Russell. New York: Cosmopolitan Science & Art Service Company, Inc., 1942.

Aúlen, Gustav. *Christus Victor*. New York: The Macmillan Co. 1951.

Baelz, Peter. *Prayer and Providence*. New York: Seabury Press, 1968.

Barnett, Henlee H. *Christian Calling and Vocation*. Grand Rapids, Michigan: Baker House, 1965.

Beach, Waldo. "The Pattern of Providence," *Theology Today*. July 1959.

Berkouwer, G. C. *The Providence of God, Studies in Dogmatics*. Translated by Lewis B. Smedes. Grand Rapids: Wm. B. Eerdmans Publishing Company, 1952.

Blamires, Harry. *The Will and the Way, A Study of Divine Providence and Vocation*. London: S.P.C.K., 1957.

Boettner, Loraine. *The Reformed Doctrine of Predestination*. Chapter V: "The Providence of God." Philadelphia: The Presbyterian and Reformed Publishing Company, 1963.

Bonhoeffer, Dietrich. *Letters and Papers from Prison*. New York: The Macmillan Co., 1953.

Brunner, Emil. *The Christian Doctrine of Creation and Redemption*. Vol. II: *"Dogmatics."* Philadelphia: The Westminster Press, 1952.

Bultmann, Rudolph. *Theology of the New Testament*. 2 Vols. New York: Charles Scribner's Sons, 1951-1955.

Cailliet, Emile. *The Recovery of Purpose*. New York: Harper and Brothers Publishers, 1959.

Calvin, John. *Institutes of the Christian Religion. The Library of Christian Classics,* ed. John T. McNeill, Vol. XX and XXI. Philadelphia: The Westminster Press, 1960.

D'arcy, Charles Frederick. *Providence and the World Order*. New York: Round Table Press, Inc., n.d.

D'arcy, M. D. *The Pain of This World and the Providence of God*. New York: Longmans, Green and Company, 1935.

Davies, D. R. *Divine Judgment in Human History.* London: Sheldon Press, 1943.

Dodd, C. H. "The Epistle of Paul to the Romans," *The Moffatt New Testament Commentary.* New York: Harper and Brothers, 1932.

———. *The Apostolic Preaching and Its Development.* London: Hodder & Stoughton Limited, 1944.

Elliott-Binns, L. E. *Divine Providence and Human Destiny.* New York: The Macmillan Co., 1943.

Farmer, H. H. *The World and God.* London: Nisbet & Company, Ltd., 1935.

Farrar, Austin. *Finite and Infinite, a Philosophical Essay.* Westminster: Dacre Press, 1943.

———. *The Freedom of the Will.* New York: Charles Scribner's Sons, 1958.

———. *Love Almighty and Ills Unlimited, An Essay on Providence and Evil, Containing the Nathaniel Taylor Lectures for 1961.* Garden City: Doubleday & Company, Inc., 1961.

Fitch, William. *God and Evil, Studies in the Mystery of Suffering and Pain.* Grand Rapids: Wm. B. Eerdmans Publishing Company, 1967.

Fletcher, Joseph. *Moral Responsibility.* Philadelphia: The Westminster Press, 1967.

———. *Situation Ethics.* Philadelphia: The Westminster Press, 1966.

Frankl, Viktor E. *Man's Search for Meaning, An Introduction to Logotherapy.* Boston: Beacon Press, 1959.

Garrigo-Lagrange, Reginald. *Providence.* Translated by Dom Bede Rose. Saint Louis: B. Herder Book Company, 1937; reprinted, 1957.

Geach, Peter. *Providence and Evil.* Cambridge: Cambridge University Press, 1977.

Gilkey, Langdon. *Maker of Heaven and Earth.* Garden City: Doubleday & Company, Inc., 1959.

———. *Reaping the Whirlwind.* New York: Seabury Press, 1976.

Griffin, David Ray. *God, Power, and Evil: A Process Theodicy.* Philadelphia: The Westminster Press, 1976.

Harkness, Georgia. *The Providence of God.* New York: Abingdon Press, 1960.

Hazelton, Roger. *Providence.* London: SCM Press, Ltd., 1958. (First published as *God's Way with Man.* Nashville: Abingdon Press, 1956.)

———. *Providence, A Theme with Variations.* London: SCM Press, Ltd., 1958.

Hick, John. *Evil and the God of Love.* London: MacMillan and Company, Ltd., 1966.

Kierkegaard, Soren. *Purity of Heart Is to Will One Thing.* London: Fontana Books, 1961.

Lewis, C. S. *The Problem of Pain.* London: The Centenary Press, 1940.

Lewis, Edwin. *The Creator and the Adversary.* New York and Nashville: Abingdon-Cokesbury Press, 1948.

McLarry, Newman R. *His Good and Perfect Will*. Nashville: Broadman Press, 1965.

McNeill, Robert. *God Wills Us Free*. New York: Hill and Wang, 1965.

Maritain, Jacques. *God and the Permission of Evil*. Translated by Joseph W. Evans. Milwaukee: Bruce Publishing Company, 1966.

Maston, T. B. *God's Will and Your Life*. Nashville: Broadman Press, 1964.

Matthews, W. R. *The Purpose of God*. Long: Nisbet and Company, Ltd., 1935; reprinted, London: Unwin Brothers, Ltd., 1936 and 1937.

Michalson, Carl. *The Hinge of History*. New York: Charles Scribner's Sons, 1959.

Morgan, G. Campbell. *God's Perfect Will*. London: Marshall Morgan & Scott, Ltd., n.d.

Nelson, Marion H. M. D. *How to Know God's Will*. Chicago: Moody Press, 1963.

Niebuhr. Reinhold. *Justice and Mercy*. Edited by Ursula M. Niebuhr. New York: Harper and Row, Publishers, n.d.

————. *The Nature and Destiny of Man*. New York: Charles Scribner's Sons, 1941.

Nygren, Anders. *Commentary on Romans*. Philadelphia: Muhlenberg Press, 1949.

Oden, Thomas C. *Radical Obedience, The Ethics of Rudolf Bultmann*. Philadelphia: The Westminster Press, 1964.

Pittenger, William Norman. *God's Way with Men*. London: Hodder & Stoughton, Ltd., 1969.

Pollard, William G. *Chance and Providence, God's Action in a World Governed by Scientific Law*. New York: Charles Scribner's Sons, 1958.

Robinson, H. Wheeler. *Suffering, Human and Divine*. London: Student Christian Movement Press, 1940.

Sanday, William and Arthur C. Headlam. *The Epistle to the Romans*. New York: Charles Scribner's Sons, n.d.

Schilling, S. Paul. *God and Human Anguish*. Nashville: Abingdon Press, 1977.

Smith, M. Blaine. *Knowing God's Will*. Downers Grove: InterVarsity Press, 1979.

Stewart, James S. *A Man in Christ*. New York: Harper and Brothers Publishers, n.d.

Sutcliffe, Edmund F. *Providence and Suffering in the Old and New Testaments*. London: Thomas Nelson and Sons, Ltd., 1953.

Telford, John. *Man's Partnership with Divine Providence*. London: Epworth Press, n.d.

Von Rad, Gerhard. *Genesis, A Commentary*. Philadelphia: The Westminster Press, 1961.

Weatherhead, Leslie D. *The Will of God*. New York: Abingdon Press, 1944.

————. *Why Do Men Suffer?* New York: Abingdon Press, 1936.

<u>Notes</u>

① Do not ask questions of a tragic loss— but ask—"What is the WILL of God from now on." Ex. Page 21

② Be patient and wait upon the Lord. We can't know His will in the beginning but we can come to know it along the pilgrimage. Page 22

③ Read the Bible along— while seeking the will of God. P. 25

④ God's will for us— is to know that others should know His light. P. 31

⑤ We shall be obediant to God. p. 31

⑥ Ask yourself— whence, whither, what, who and why.

Faith comes only when one knows a "personal trust." p. 46 which leads to loyalty.